All rights reserved. No part of this publication may be reproduced, stored in a retrieval system, or transmitted, in any form or by any means, electronic, mechanical, photocopying, recording, or otherwise without prior written permission of the publisher.

The author and publisher of the book do not make any claim or guarantee for any physical, mental, emotional, spiritual, or financial result. All products, services and information provided by the author are for general education and entertainment purposes only. The information provided herein is in no way a substitute for medical or other professional advice. In the event you use any of the information contained in this book for yourself, the author and publisher assume no responsibility for your actions.

Conscious Leadership

The Key to Unlocking Success

Published by
Access Consciousness Publishing, LLC
www.accessconsciousnesspublishing.com

Printed in the United States of America

First published in 2005 by LifeMastery (Asia.) Pty. Ltd.
Copyright © LifeMastery (Asia.) Pty Ltd.

By
Chutisa Bowman and Steven Bowman
Major Contribution by Gary M. Douglas

ACCESS
CONSCIOUSNESS®
PUBLISHING

Conscious Leadership
Copyright © 2014 Chutisa and Steven Bowman
ISBN: 978-1-939261-29-8

All rights reserved. No part of this publication may be reproduced, stored in a retrieval system, or transmitted, in any form or by any means, electronic, mechanical, photocopying, recording or otherwise without prior written permission from the publisher.

The author and publisher of the book do not make any claim or guarantee for any physical, mental, emotional, spiritual, or financial result. All products, services and information provided by the author are for general education and entertainment purposes only. The information provided herein is in no way a substitute for medical or other professional advice. In the event you use any of the information contained in this book for yourself, the author and publisher assume no responsibility for your actions.

Published by
Access Consciousness Publishing, LLC
www.accessconsciousnesspublishing.com

Printed in the United States of America

First published in 2005 by LifeMastery (Aust.) Pty. Ltd.
Copyright © LifeMastry (Aust) Pty. Ltd.

Contents

Introduction

This book is an invitation for those people who choose to be more conscious in their leadership, with an emphasis that no particular way is right or wrong. This book came about because we are dedicated to assisting people to raise their awareness and consciousness, which in turn has an expansive effect on all those who come in contact with a conscious leader.

Conscious leaders are those who are charismatic, are able to make powerful and successful decisions that defy logic and analysis, are innovative in the ways they address issues, have a major impact on the expansiveness of their organisation and the people affected by the organisation, and are defined by the key characteristic that they have followers who choose to follow them.

The vision of this book is to enable you to easily access brilliant tools of power and transformation for as many people as are ready to use them. It is our firm belief that the enhancement and expansion of consciousness is one of the most essential factors for everyday living as we move into the uncertainties of this millennium. We can enrich our lives in every aspect as we empower ourselves to be more conscious in our personal and professional lives.

~ 1 ~

The Essence of Leadership

To become an extraordinary leader, an executive must become a conscious leader by combining both executive management skills and conscious leadership abilities.

Leadership is a process of *Being* rather than *Doing*. This establishes the quality, attitude and disposition which delineates extraordinary leaders.

> *Being a leader is not the same as acting as one,*
> *and calling yourself a leader is not the same as being one.*

What do most people misidentify and misapply as leadership?

Most executives these days are appointed into leadership positions by virtue of their technical skills, knowledge and education. Seldom are people chosen to become leaders of an organisation because of their sheer leadership qualities and abilities. In most organisations, "Leaders" are in fact "Managers" working under a leadership title. Many people in management believe that they can become leaders in their organisation or field of expertise because they know so much about the business, their extensive experience in the field, superior technical knowledge and excellent process management skills. This is often not the case.

In the study of leadership, most investigators and theorists believe that managerial and leadership skills are different. A leader needs to be concerned with the big picture and the vision of an organization. Managers, on the other hand, are concerned with day-to-day routine operations. The differences can be elaborated as:

- Leaders create and articulate vision and strategy, management ensures it is put into practice through planning and budgeting

- Leadership welcomes change and opportunity, while management focuses on dealing with complexity

- Leaders embrace accountability and transparency internally and externally, while managers focus on the doing and the achieving of budget and plans

- Leaders excel at public relations, being open in their communications, sharing of information and articulation of the organisational vision, while management refers to these communications for guidance

- Leaders recognise risk as opportunity, while management ensure risks are understood and controlled

Most leadership gurus talk about leadership styles, tools and techniques for leading people. This is the most subtle misidentification and misapplication of the notion of leadership. Many of these conventional leadership models require leaders to sustain a controlled structure in which staff follow specified directives and perform them efficiently and in the approved manner. The tools and techniques that these leadership gurus often recommend are effectively the instruments that can be used to control and have power over people. These tools and techniques simply provide great psychological methods to enable the exertion of control. In this way, leadership is perceived to be power-based.

In addition, most standard leadership training programs focus exclusively on skills, and again develop managers rather than leaders. Traditional leadership models seek to preserve the status quo and make good "soldiers" of the team. These models are based in authority, hierarchy, exclusivity and separation between management and staff. It is important to recognize that it is just not possible to truly manage and control other people. Most of the time we can't even manage ourselves! It is important to recognize that it is not feasible to manage people, because people are unpredictable, uncontainable, uncontrollable, paradoxical and unruly. They can be forced to obey, but cannot be managed in the traditional sense. To become a conscious leader, it is essential to acknowledge what leadership is truly all about. It is about empowerment rather than force.

To become an extraordinary leader, an executive must become a conscious leader by combining both executive management skills and conscious leadership abilities. Executive management skills are necessary to win credibility with the staff as a leader and with the board of governance as an executive. In this framework, executive management is not about managing the people to get things done in the business, but is more to do with taking vision and strategy to the staff. It is about managing what things get done through which people.

Key Points

- Leadership is a process of *Being* rather than *Doing*.

- Conscious Leadership is about empowerment rather than force.

- Being a leader is not the same as acting as one, and calling yourself a leader is not the same as being one.

- To become an extraordinary leader, an executive must become a conscious leader by combining both executive management skills and conscious leadership abilities.

~ 2 ~

The Spirit of Conscious Leadership

*A conscious leader is the source of an organisation's success,
joy, glory and prosperity.*

Many theories of leadership have discussed leadership in terms of "nature" (i.e., you are born with leadership qualities or not) or "nurture" (i.e., leadership is a teachable skill). In accordance with the understanding that everything in our universe is energy, and that we all have access to this "oneness" of energy, we posit that everyone has the ability to be an extraordinary leader; it is all about the choices that people make.

The key to becoming an extraordinary leader is "consciousness"—the talents and abilities that we already have but have not claimed, owned, acknowledged and embraced. Consciousness is our intrinsic faculty and inner resource; however, for most people it has been concealed and undeveloped. The truth is we are all equal, we are infinite beings. We have consciousness, we are consciousness and we have a choice to be consciousness.

It is important to be aware of and acknowledge that everyone has infinite potential to be a conscious leader, because we all are infinite beings. Consciousness resides inside each of us as an infinite reservoir of intuitive knowing, wisdom and acumen. If claimed, owned and embraced wholeheartedly, sincerely and ardently, "consciousness" allows leaders to revel in their own greatness and extraordinariness without superiority or hierarchy. When leaders choose consciousness, those around them share the rewards (this is the phenomenon of entrainment, described in Chapter 3). A conscious leader is the source of an organization's success, joy, glory and prosperity.

People who choose leadership or who are given the opportunity to be a leader, have three choices that they can make. They can choose to be a Conscious leader, an Unconscious leader, or an Anti-conscious leader. To become extraordinary leaders all they have to do is choose "consciousness." Consciousness is a choice, just as unconscious and anti-conscious are choices. People begin to become conscious leaders at the moment when they choose for themselves to be conscious.

Conscious leadership is about right here, right now. It is the moment you choose to be all that is possible.

φ φ φ

Being Conscious

Consciousness is correlated to the intensity of one's connection with oneself, with one's acceptance of unlimited talents and abilities and the resulting expansion of one's ability to be in communion with all things.

Being conscious is an experience of expanding our awareness beyond its present limits. It is a state of flexible awareness, with no fixed points of view. The basic function of each being is **expanding** and **contracting.** Expanded beings are lightness, infiniteness and indefinable; contracted beings are solid mass, density and limitation. A completely expanded being is what we call a **conscious being.** When we are completely expanded, we have a feeling of total awareness, of being one with life; that place where we have a stillness, a sense of total peace and tranquility, in which we have no capacity to judge. Living in that reality means that we allow all of life to come to us with ease, joy and glory. Being conscious is the very process of expansion; it has nothing to do with new age concepts, the latest fads, or any *should* or *shouldn't* beliefs.

φ φ φ

Conscious Leaders

Conscious leaders are creative innovators who can function from total perceiving, knowing, being and receiving. They have the ability to transcend their limited circumstances and to actualize infinite possibilities. They create their reality by choosing to let go of limitations and demand of themselves the greatness of who they are. They are not attached to convention or past reference points, and are always willing to take risks and destroy and un-create old systems, structures and routines for new ones. They live not as the effect of life, but as the source of it. Conscious leaders stand out from the crowd.

Conscious leaders have a strong penchant for innovation, they believe in infinite possibilities, they seek and maximize opportunity and are able to perceive and work with risk. They live in simultaneity (time, space and reality all at the same time), they tend to look at the big picture of things and see the big picture of things all the time. Conscious leaders operate on inner knowing and use intuition for making expansive decisions. They are influential, inspirational and provide visions that transform the way people think about what is possible, feasible and attainable. Conscious leaders are comfortable with change, they understand that the status quo is an oxymoron, that there is simply no such thing. Every minute, every day, there is change—things are in constant motion. While others may not be aware of this, conscious leaders live it. In knowing that change is inevitable, the conscious leader seeks change for a purpose, for the better. They have the ability to change their point of view constantly and without judgment.

The culture of an organisation that has a conscious leader is characterized by a focus on integrity, trust, creativity, intuition, innovation, freedom, flexibility and generosity. The culture is one which searches to create conditions for cohesion, community spirit, and mutual accountability, and that recognizes the importance of strategic alliances with suppliers and customers (corporate well being). There is a shift from control to trust, fear to truth, privilege to equality, and fragmentation to unity.

φ φ φ

Unconscious Leaders
Unconscious leaders are typically appointed to their position as CEO, manager or supervisor. Due to their position of authority, they become

the Boss and have the power that allows them to be in command of and direct their staff. Staff would not necessarily voluntarily follow *the Boss* in the normal course of events, but are expected to carry out directions and obey the dictums of *the Boss*.

Unconscious leaders often get appointed into their position because of their expertise in their field, many of whom have worked their way up the hierarchy. They often possess good technical information and knowledge of the system that can make best use of resources and maximize organizational productivity.

The unconscious leader will make many decisions and generally is quite busy being busy, but is unaware of what has influenced those decisions, actions or feelings. They are skilled at providing constancy, following rules, maintaining the status quo and cultivating order in the organisation. Unconscious leaders tend to focus on the process and immediate efficiency. They are generally inclined to blame most problems on external forces, and feel that luck, outside events, other people or fate often have an influence on their current situation, and that what they now have is possibly as good as it gets. The more unconscious they are, the more risk-averse they become. Their common phrases include *but, just, need, try, want* and *never*.

These unconscious leaders are seeking more in life, home and work, but are unsure what or how to effect change. Things happen around them, often leaving them bemused and worried.

The culture created by an unconscious leader is characterized by hierarchical power structures, a strong emphasis on quality and process, very busy being busy with a general unawareness of what is influencing decisions, actions and feelings related to the results, a general lack of creativity and an unwillingness to uncreate and destroy form and structure.

φ φ φ

Anti-conscious Leaders

There are those leaders who actively work against the consciousness of themselves and those around them. They create conflict and discord, are often status and power hungry, and tend to want to build empires and actively play office politics. They work long hours (and expect others to as well) and neglect their life and families. They create points of view that are very contractive to themselves, their family and their organisation. These are the anti-conscious leaders.

They do not allow the free flow of information (performance, financials, strategy etc), and have such fixed points of view that allow for no other possibilities. Their concrete mindset can also cause them to discern others as adversaries and to justify reprisal against them. They often struggle to alleviate their insecurity thorough excessive control and territorial behaviour. The environment within their organisation (and at home) is toxic. The anti-conscious leader creates unhealthy climates in their organisation. The anti-conscious leader works very hard at creating their reality so it is not ease or joy for themselves or those around them.

The culture created by an anti-conscious leader is typically autocratic, uncaring, fear driven with attempts to control everything. There is a general underlying fear of invalidation and reprisals, and a distinct lack of sharing of information. The culture is one of what is right or wrong, good or bad, and is typified by the "you are either with me or against me" point of view.

Key Points

- Being conscious is the very process of expansion; it has nothing to do with new age concepts or the latest fads or beliefs.

- Living in that reality means that we allow all of life to come to us with ease, joy and glory.

- Consciousness is a choice, just as unconscious and anti-conscious are choices. Leaders can choose to be conscious, unconscious, or anti-conscious.

- When leaders choose against consciousness, they are choosing anti-conscious.

~ 3 ~

Why Would Leaders Choose to Be Conscious?

Conscious leaders emanate an energy field of healing, nurturing, caring, joyfulness, fun, expansiveness and an intensity of infiniteness.

- Imagine that all of life comes to you with ease, joy and glory. Glory is an exuberant expression of life and abundance in all things.

- Imagine being able to make decisions effortlessly and being able to resolve problems and dissolve conflict with ease.

- Imagine your life is permeated and saturated with insight and energy.

This is the power of Consciousness.

φ φ φ

Gary Douglas of Access Consciousness® states—"Healing, Caring, Nurturing, Creativity, Joyfulness, Fun, Expansiveness and Intensity of Infiniteness are the expressions of a perennial pure conscious essence." This is the essence of who you truly are. When you are *in the flow*, where things are in harmony and in sync, you have transformed from a state of unconsciousness to consciousness. Your actions and purposes are matched, and the outcomes are dynamic, creative, efficient and rewarding. Conscious leaders emanate an energy field of healing, nurturing, caring, joyfulness, fun, expansiveness and an intensity of infiniteness.

Consciousness is our intrinsic faculty and inner resource. However, the majority of people are so disconnected from their own states of consciousness that they are not aware that it is possible to actually experience this state. For most people, everyday living is a struggle. However, we all have an inner urge toward living more naturally with ease, which is free of disharmony, trauma and drama. Yet within us also resides a strong attachment to anti-conscious habits from our past programming. This attachment to anti-conscious habits causes us to be quite disconnected from our own infinite possibilities. We have been impacted with so many external thoughts, beliefs, attitudes, energies, limitations and negativity that we are not able to perceive, know, be and receive that we are that infinite possibility. We are not aware that it is possible to actually experience this state. Unconsciously, most people do not even realize that the state of pure consciousness is the true essence of their Beingness. A downbeat self depiction often obstructs the joyous exuberant expression and abundance of life that is the true essence of their Beingness (pure consciousness).

Ultimately, consciousness is a way of connecting what is happening at the present moment with the infinite possibilities. Conscious leaders constantly experience the abundance of life itself and the privilege of life itself because they are able to perceive, know, be and receive that wherever they are, just by the power of energy that is their true being, anything is possible. And this is a most glorious and magnificent place to be.

In consciousness all of life happens with Ease, Joy and Glory. You would NOT choose consciousness for what reason?

A conscious leader brings a sense of purpose to an organization. Conscious leaders set directions, whereas unconscious leaders look to others for direction. Where the conscious leader motivates others to achieve a shared target by example or power of presence, the unconscious leader disperses duties and scrutinizes progress in their achievement. Where the conscious leader accepts authority to achieve a target, unconscious leaders allot authority and accept instruction in its application and use. Unconscious leaders keep an organization functioning; whereas conscious leaders focus on why the organization exists, where it is going and what it would take to expand and enhance it.

Conscious leaders have the ability to choose with awareness that which brings joy and expansiveness to them and others.

φ φ φ

Harmonic Coherence

Conscious Leaders have an energetic empowerment presence which creates an energy field of healing, nurturing, caring, creativity, expansiveness, and joyfulness. This energy field has what is known as a harmonic coherence frequency which strongly affects others around the conscious leader. This is the source of the conscious leaders' vibrational energy, commonly known as magnetism or charisma. This harmonic coherence frequency has been shown to have an almost telepathic effect on others and on the environment. The most common manifestations of this harmonic coherence are evidenced through comments such as "How did you know I was going to do that?", "I was just about to say that," "I knew that was going to happen," "When we are in the zone, it's like we can read each others minds."

Recent scientific research, including chaos theory and quantum mechanics, has shown that everything and everyone in the universe, every thought and every attitude gives off a vibration, a frequency, and that they are all connected through energy. We all are broadcasting stations radiating our energetic signals to the world. Each person has a particular frequency or vibration—a consciousness or energetic signal, which we radiate or transmit to the environment and other people. It is a composite of the particular frequency or vibration of our body, our mind, our heart, and our consciousness. Each being has the ability to control their own vibration. Just as you adjust your radio to a particular station by adjusting its frequency, you can attune to higher energetic vibrations by expanding your consciousness.

φ φ φ

Harmonic Coherence and Entrainment

This harmonic coherence also affects other people in a multitude of ways through a process known as entrainment. Entrainment can be defined as the tendency for two oscillating bodies to lock into phase so that they vibrate in harmony (harmonic coherence). The principle of entrainment is universal, appearing in music, biology, chemistry, pharmacology, medicine, psychology, sociology, astronomy, architecture and many other disciplines.

The history of entrainment is linked to findings of the Dutch scientist Christian Huygens in 1665. While working on the design of the pendulum clock, Huygens found that when he placed two of them on a wall near each other and swung the pendulums at different rates, they would eventually end up swinging at the same rate. This also occurred when a room was filled with grandfather clocks, all of different sizes and different pendulum lengths, and each was set swinging. The clocks become synchronized with each other by sending and receiving minute vibrations through the walls and floor of the building. Not only was energy being transferred, but the individual clocks themselves altered their *behavior* in order to become synchronized with the other clocks. Equally noteworthy is the fact that the slower clocks picked up their pace to become synchronized with the fastest (highest frequency) clock. This *entrainment* process has been replicated over and over through the centuries, and has given rise to many scientific and arts-related disciplines.

φ φ φ

Expansion and Contraction

The fundamental function of each being is expanding and contracting their consciousness. Leaders always have the experiences and perceptions appropriate to their vibration level. When leaders are totally expanded, they have a perception of full awareness, of being in communion with all of life. However, when they are totally contracted they become unconscious, energy dense and resisting everyone and everything. Unconscious leaders feel anxious and apprehensive and are filled with worry and self-doubt when they are highly contracted. Anti-conscious leaders choose this state and revel in it.

When leaders expand their intensity of consciousness, they expand their energetic empowerment and create a stirring of "Harmonic Coherence" throughout the organisation. An elevated intensity of consciousness allows the leader to make an authentic communion with people. In the state of unconscious or anti-conscious, there is no communion, only separation. When leaders are unconscious or anti-conscious they are living and functioning in a state of separation from the wholeness of life. It takes a great deal of energy to be functioning in the state of unconscious or anti-conscious. This misuse of energy is a toxic and harmful force in personal and work life.

Key Points

- Consciousness is a way of connecting what is happening at the present with the infinite possibilities.

- Expanding personal consciousness creates a harmonic coherence frequency resulting in entrainment of people throughout the organisation.

- Conscious leaders emanate an energy field of healing, nurturing, caring, joyfulness, fun, expansiveness and an intensity of infiniteness.

~ 4 ~

Conscious Leaders
Live and Operate from
BEINGNESS

Conscious leaders embrace infinite possibilities and live from total
PERCEIVING, KNOWING, BEING,
and RECEIVING.

The key point about consciousness is that "You have consciousness, you are consciousness and you have a choice to be consciousness." You have to choose to be consciousness, it's not a place you go to—it is who you are. To be a conscious leader, you must choose to be a conscious leader; you must claim, own and acknowledge it and have it in you. That which you do not have in you, you cannot have at all. If you see consciousness as external and not part of your beingness, you will never have it at all. It is your own withdrawal from awareness, your own mass condition that creates separation and contraction.

Conscious leaders live and operate from BEINGNESS, from the extraordinariness and the limitless that they are, from the infinite possibilities that exist. They embrace infinite possibilities and live from total PERCEIVING, KNOWING, BEING, and RECEIVING. When leaders live and function from total perceiving, knowing, being and receiving, they become true allowance, void of judgment and fear.

Perceiving, Knowing, Being, and Receiving

Conscious leaders perceive, know, be and receive their greatness and claim and own their infiniteness. They relate to life in spontaneous interaction with the energy of the moment and have the ability to perceive, know, be and receive everything.

Perceiving: Perceiving is about being aware of the energy of everything that is occurring. Conscious leaders have the ability to perceive all that is happening around them, including thoughts, biases and feelings, without buying into that perception as reality. They are aware of what is happening around and within them and their organisations, they observe without judgment, they are willing to experience without form, structure or significance, and they function from a space where everything is *just an interesting point of view*, rather than aligning and agreeing, or resisting and reacting. In total perceiving, the conscious leader can enjoy both the beauty and the beast without any judgment and is able to see it as just an interesting point of view.

Practical...Perceiving

- What you are unwilling to perceive, or when you have decided that you *can't have* something, then these have already defined you and have become the limitation of who you are.

- You cannot be totally expansive without the willingness to be or to perceive everything. You are an infinite being, and everything is available and possible.

Knowing: Knowing is the intelligent flow of insight and knowledge that transpires instantaneously once the mind and emotions are balanced, calm and coherent. It is a dimension of consciousness far deeper than thought. Knowing has nothing to do with the thinking mind; it is not a product of thought. Functioning from *Knowing* is not implemented through hard labor nor is it executed through force and exertion. It occurs by following the energy. Following the energy is about asking questions so that the universe and your inner knowing (intuition) have an avenue for responding. Conscious leaders are empowered to know that they know, as they are able to connect with their inner knowing. They empower themselves with the awareness of the fact that they know everything, they acknowledge that they know and that every time they validate their knowing, they increase their knowing. Conscious leaders choose to know instantaneously, to have an aware presence, where intuition is embraced as powerful and insightful, and where they have moved from trying to be *in the head,* to trusting in their own knowing. Conscious leaders never say "I don't know," but rather say "I don't have an answer for this at the moment," or "I don't have a point of view on this at the moment." Whenever they are required to know anything, all they have to do is to follow the energy and ask to know.

Practical...Knowing

- Knowing has nothing to do with the thinking mind; it is not a product of thought.

- When you are "thinking" and "in your head," you are not functioning from your Knowing

Being: Being is about relating to life in spontaneous interaction with the energy of the moment, without thought, without intention, without desire or consideration of the next moment. Conscious leaders are able to be all and everything simultaneously without judgment, competition, separation, discrimination and discernment; they are living life from the point of view of celebration everyday. Conscious leaders are being an invitation for the abundant universe to provide them with infinite opportunities. They are totally present, able to function in the simultaneity of past, present and future and thus not be influenced unconsciously by past events or future concerns. They live in the question, rather than being besieged by the problems. They know how to ask questions in a more unlimited way in which they allow the answers that they hadn't considered as possibilities, to manifest. Choosing to be is where the conscious leader chooses to lead life by living in "10 second increments" and making conscious choices every 10 seconds (see Chapter 6).

Practical…Being

- Living life from the point of view of celebration every day

- Being grateful for who you are. Appreciate how extraordinary you are and claim and own the freedom of having no point of view about you.

- Do everything from INVITATION instead of force.

Receiving: Receiving is the key component for expanding consciousness. Receiving involves *no resistance;* it is about remaining constantly open, vulnerable and unresisting to any energy. Conscious leaders are willing to receive everything that can come into their life and having no resistance in their awareness and their mind. They are willing to receive the greatness of who they are, which opens the door for others to choose to be more conscious. They are able to receive all with true gratitude without any sense of obligation, judgment or filtering. They do not resist or react to any interaction with anything or anyone. They recognize that whatever they can't receive becomes a limitation. Whenever leaders are unwilling to receive certain energies, they are functioning from separation, judgment, expectation, projection, and rejection. When leaders are unwilling to receive, they withdraw from being in communion with others and from all things.

Practical...Receiving

- Be willing to receiving everything that can come into your life, including the judgment of others.

- Look at what you are not willing to receive in your life. What you are unwilling to receive will limit the amount you can have in your life.

- At the bottom of any problem is an unwillingness to receive. If you are not happy and contented, look first at what you are unwilling to receive in your life. When your life is not working as well as you would like, there is always something you are not willing to receive.

~ 5 ~

Evolving Leadership to
Conscious Leadership

Conscious leadership is a process of "Being" rather than "Doing."
Conscious leadership is about empowerment
rather than having the power over.

What do leaders have to do to become conscious leaders?
What are the signs that they are succeeding?

Conscious leadership is not just about learning to be a leader; it is about allowing your authentic inner leadership qualities to come forth. Conscious leadership has to do with a new sense of equilibrium and balance:

- between inner and outer leadership,

- between personal growth and business growth,

- between embracing the vision and empowering others to achieve it,

- between the head and the heart.

What do "Conscious Leadership" qualities look like?

Conscious leadership is about empowerment rather than having the power over. Empowerment is about encouraging the consciousness of others. Conscious leadership is a process of *Being* rather than *Doing*. To encourage the spirit of others requires many diverse qualities.

- **Intuition** – Heightened awareness, the ability to stay totally present, attentive and proactive. Conscious leaders are masters at managing through ambiguity.

- **Insightful** – Attune to that which has not yet manifested and let the infinite possibilities work for them. Conscious leaders have a knowing that is not limited in any way by time, space and physicality.

- **Inspirational** – Ability to perceive unlimited potential and inspire others with their vision. Conscious leaders are able to perceive, know, be and receive phenomena from many different tangible and intangible levels.

- **Innovation** – Recognize and trust change. Conscious leaders build a culture of consciousness that embraces change.

- **Influential** – Conscious leaders influence through personal power.

What would it take to evolve from leadership to conscious leadership?

To evolve from leadership to conscious leadership, leaders must have a sincerity and willingness to be conscious leaders, and they must demand of themselves to choose consciousness, no matter what it takes. The first question that leaders must ask themselves is *"Do I have a sincere aspiration and willingness to be a conscious leader?"* The answer can only be *yes* or *no*, because wishful desire does not provide a fertile inner ecology required for consciousness to expand. Sincerity and willingness are essential, because they facilitate consciousness to expand its possibilities by motivating the leader to demand of themselves to choose consciousness.

What would it be like if you could function as the infiniteness of you instead of the finiteness of you?

For an individual to evolve from leadership to conscious leadership requires overcoming previous *unconscious conditioning*. This conditioning has fundamentally taught and implanted *the typical human point of view of thoughts, feelings, emotions, and finiteness*. In this reality, the finite place people function from is thoughts, feelings and emotions. It is essential to recognise that thoughts, feelings and emotions are a byproduct of the mind, which is a regulating system of our life. The mind is a calculating system that is only here to define what we already are familiar with; it defines the limitations of our reality. The mind gets in the way of knowing because it justifies everything leaders do and does nothing to create infinite possibilities. The mind induces leaders to function from a limited point of view and define everything according to a linear point of view that is a solid physical mode, in order to conform to long-established human perspectives. It is essential to recognize that most of the trauma, suffering, distress and great effort which occurs in unconscious and anti-conscious leaders' lives originates from their restricted ability to perceive beyond parameters of finite and limited human perspectives. Unconscious leaders are contracted not because of the dismal circumstances they are in; they are in dismal circumstances because they have chosen contraction and chosen to function in a scarcity paradigm.

This *unconscious conditioning* has created limitation in leaders' lives by limiting what they can perceive, know, be and receive, and forced leaders to function unconsciously. This typical human point of view has conditioned leaders to believe that they need to create their reality and their lives from judgment and that they could not simply do it from choice and beingness. The judgments are held in place by the leaders' personal viewpoints, decisions they have made and any points of view that are fixed. When leaders create their lives from judgment, they tend to do everything unconsciously or anti-consciously with force, effort, density, decision and violence. The *unconscious conditioning* mesmerizes leaders into an unconscious state and sets leaders up to automatically go into judgment, discrimination and discernment. Whenever leaders make a judgment about anything, those things that do not match their judgment cannot come into their universe. Judgment keeps leaders finite, limited, diminished, separate, and destroys their ability to function from choice and beingness. When functioning in this state of *unconscious conditioning* leaders cannot have perceiving, knowing, being and receiving except in limited quantity.

This *unconscious conditioning* is what keeps leaders in a polarized reality, as it sustains leaders in a linear concept of being, rather than in simultaneity. This creates the polarization and lower harmonics of leaders' lives (polarization is the positive and negative, the black and the white, the right and the wrong, alignment and agreement to someone or something, or the resistance and reaction to a person or situation in life). Living in this reality means that leaders will constantly create trauma and drama in their lives; this is because they are addicted to polarity. Leaders are solely responsible for the condition of their lives and for everything that happens to them. They create everything themselves.

> **Leaders are the creator of everything that is expansive
> and everything that is contracted about their lives.**

Everything that leaders are, they have created. In one way or another, leaders create everything that they have in their life that doesn't work or is not so good (i.e., relationship problems, work predicaments, physical malady, pain, discomfort, financial dilemmas etc). Leaders create these through their thoughts, feelings, emotions, and through their spoken words.

The key step is to be conscious and aware, being precise in what leaders think and what they speak, because exactly what they think and speak is what they will create. As leaders think and as leaders speak they create a vibration. Every thought and every word has a vibration, an electrical energetic component which creates leaders' reality. These will be exactly the parameters from which leaders will be creating their life. Every time a leader thinks "I am……..," that is exactly what they become. If leaders think that they are worthless, they are going to create a low self regard and miserable life. If leaders think that they feel disempowered, they are going to feel dismal, pathetic and contracted. If leaders' thinking is based on scarcity and lack, they will always have no abundance.

Is it any wonder that the bulk of people subsist in a scarcity paradigm? Not realizing it, they choose to believe in *lack of* and "there is not enough to go around." They fail to recognize that they possess the great power to choose.

So, it is crucial to acknowledge that the things and the state of affairs in a leaders' life are thoughts first, before they develop into reality. For example, their financial condition and their existence is a thought first, and then manifests into a reality. If leaders want to have a more expansive existence and abundant financial picture, they must first look at their thoughts and consciously choose more expansive thoughts. Leaders have to take responsibility for what they think and what they say. The responsibility is "I am creating this" and "I have the power to choose." The greatest power that a person possesses is the power to choose with awareness. When conscious leaders function with awareness, they don't have any thought, just awareness. Awareness allows them to function with no density, so choices can be made instantaneously.

In essence, anything which is any form of pain, suffering, trauma, drama, or limitation in a leaders' life is created by them through aligning and agreeing or resisting and reacting to it. If things are not good in their life, leaders have to look for where they have chosen to be unconscious and have not chosen with awareness. To create the polarized reality they currently have, leaders have to be unconscious and unwilling to claim and own their ability to perceive, know, be and receive everything. Unconscious leaders have been conditioned to accept as true *that's just the way life is, there is no other choice and nothing can be any different no matter what you do. It's just going to end up the same way anyway, so why bother trying to change it?* Unconscious leaders have chosen to be the effect of life, not the cause of life.

> *The good news is that leaders, and leaders alone,*
> *have the power to transform and recreate their lives,*
> *and leaders can choose to do so at any moment.*

Leaders need to start looking at all the distress and dissonance they have created in their lives. Once they can claim what a great commotion they have created, and how powerful they are to have created such great turmoil in their lives, they can choose to create something different and create something wonderful. As leaders claim, own and acknowledge that they are fully responsible for all the experiences they have had to this point in their lives, what they are also claiming and acknowledging is that they have the power to take total control of their lives from now on. It takes more power to create our life as a disaster, than it does to create it as magnificent.

To overcome previous *unconscious conditioning*, first and foremost leaders need to empower themselves with the awareness that they perceive, know, be and receive everything. *Perceiving, Knowing, Being* and *Receiving* are the four things that an infinite being does (see Chapter 4). If leaders are doing anything else, they are operating out of finiteness not infiniteness. **To become fully conscious, leaders need to claim, own and acknowledge that they have power to create their lives from choice and beingness** and let go of the urge to create their lives from judgment, expectation, projection, separation and rejection. They must be willing to give up everything that they think is the best of this polarized reality, and must be willing to create a life that is greater than what they now have.

For leaders to create their lives from choice and beingness, they must function from their knowing and awareness, and must be willing to function from no fixed point of view. A fixed point of view creates limitation because whenever leaders have a fixed point of view, they try to defend it. The moment leaders try to defend anything, they are no longer free to choose. When leaders are functioning from knowing and awareness they become unlimited; they are not restricted in any way by time, space or physicality. They are able to perceive, know, be, receive and spontaneously discern phenomena from many different tangible and indefinable levels. To fully function from knowing, leaders must be willing to live in the moment, without linear cause and effect and must be willing to risk all pretended stability and safety in all their relationships and circumstances of life.

Knowing is not a product of thought. Functioning from knowing means leaders must stop identifying with their thinking mind because the thinking mind is only a small aspect of the consciousness that they are. When the mind is immersed in compulsive thinking, leaders cannot get in touch with their deeper knowing. It is important to recognise that a fixed point of view, prejudice and judgment of any kind implies that leaders are identifying with the thinking mind. The deep knowing that is intuition arises through the simple act of giving their full attention to whatever leaders are doing and being in the moment. Attention dissolves the barriers created by conceptual thought. When leaders function from their knowing they make no effort, they just choose. Conscious leaders follow the energy and choose based on what's going to be most expansive for them and for everyone concerned.

φ φ φ

Conscious Leadership is not about superiority or competition.

Being conscious does not make leaders more superior, it just makes them more aware. With awareness, conscious leaders can know the potential future, they can perceive the possibilities, they can perceive the limitations and they can see everything that's going to happen. When leaders are totally aware, they will not be an effect of anyone else's unconsciousness or anti-consciousness. What differentiates the conscious leader from an unconscious or anti-conscious leader is that the conscious leader doesn't have the necessity of proving that they are more superior or are greater than anyone else. Unconscious and anti-conscious leaders often *do* superiority because they are always trying to prove that they are not inferior and that they have value.

Are superiority and competition real, or does it mean unconscious and anti-conscious leaders are unable to know the value of who they are?

Conscious leaders function from beingness, from the greatness that they are, from the infinite possibilities that can exist, therefore they don't have a need to compete with or compare themselves to anyone. Unconscious and anti-conscious leaders, on the other hand, often feel the need to compete in business and in life because they operate in the scarcity paradigm of not enough, and because they feel less about themselves. Competing against others always entails judgments or comparisons with perceived rivals, which is an expression of implanted fears. They feel that there is not enough to go around or too little of everything: opportunities, prospects, support, resources, time and money. Leaders who feel the need to compete do not claim and own the greatness that they are. They are always feeling insecure and less than. It is important to recognize that if leaders take a point of view on competition, leaders cannot and will not be greater than their competitors. If defeating competitors is the only way leaders can be successful and feel good about themselves, leaders are reliant on their competitors. In other words, their competitors have power over them.

There is no such thing as competition when conscious leaders create themselves from the infiniteness, from the greatness that they are. As the infinite being that they truly are, conscious leaders celebrate their colleagues and other groups being successful in their business ventures. Conscious leaders would say, *"It is fantastic that these people are doing so well. What would it take for it to show up in my life."* Unconscious and anti-conscious leaders would say, *"How come they got it and I didn't?"*

The perceived threats of competitors often dominate the unconscious and anti-conscious leaders' thoughts and business approaches. They are always trying to defeat the other people and defend themselves against the perceived danger of being taken advantage of, being ripped off, or losing. They don't trust people and often evaluate others in terms of what level of threat these people pose to their success. Unconscious leaders would say *"I am concerned that these people will rip me off, I had better be careful about sharing information and I had better come up with a strategy to protect myself against my competitors."* Anti-conscious leaders would say *"I am afraid that these people pose a business risk to me and perhaps if I discredit or ruin them, they will be less of a potential threat to me."* Conscious Leaders would say *"How can I work with the others to create an expansion for us and everyone concerned, and how does it get any better than this?"*

When leaders choose to function in a scarcity and competition paradigm, they destroy their ability to receive from everything in the universe, which means they limit the success they can have in their life and in the organisation they lead. They limit the money they can have, they limit the people they can have in their lives, they limit the awareness they can have, they limit the power they can have, and will stay stuck in the complexity of their thoughts, feelings and emotions. As long as leaders hold on to the point of view that they need to be in competition with others, they deny the power they have to create their own success and allow their competitors to have power over them. Conscious leaders know that competitors can only steal or take from them, those things that match the leaders' limitations. The conscious leader knows that when they create themselves and their business from infinite possibilities and greatness, then no one can match what they have created and there is no competition. Conscious leaders are willing to be outstanding in what they do.

~ 6 ~

Harnessing
Conscious Leadership

*To harness conscious leadership, leaders must choose to claim and
own their true self which is an unlimited and infinite being, and
become a creator of their own life.*

Everything is choice. Everything is infinite possibility.
Everything is the question. Nothing is the answer.

—G. D., Access Consciousness

Conscious leadership is only a matter of choice. If leaders choose to be conscious, then they can be. If they choose to be unconscious or anti-conscious, then they can be that as well. With the power to choose, leaders can choose to experience unity and peace, or isolation and fear. At any moment, leaders can individually and collectively affect the course of their lives by choosing to direct their attention to the aspect of themselves which is conscious—and through the practice of choosing, to expand their awareness. The choice to expand instead of contract is ultimately a leaders' most powerful tool and freedom. To totally expand, it is crucial to have no alignment or agreement with anyone's point of view, no resistance to anyone's point of view, no reaction to anyone's point of view including their own fixed point of view. A leaders' choice of expanding awareness affects not only their own perceptions and experiences, but also the experiences and behaviors of others.

The key to harnessing conscious leadership involves a shift in the way leaders function in the world and the way leaders perceive and create their reality. It is fundamental for leaders to recognise and acknowledge that they are not their story or their personal history. Leaders need to recognize that they create themselves and their realities exactly as their thought pattern which gets accrued in the mind and body, and is expressed as incoherence, turmoil, stress, and fear in their lives. This is not who they truly are. To harness conscious leadership, leaders must choose to claim and own their true self which is an unlimited and infinite being, and become a creator of their own life. While there are no rules for doing this, there are tools and techniques to help leaders develop and expand their conscious leadership qualities.

This chapter explores nine elements of conscious leadership that leaders can choose to cultivate within their being if they are to connect with their own states of pure consciousness, so that infinite possibilities and conscious leadership can become their way of being in the world. Access Consciousness tools have been presented here to help leaders cultivate each quality. Use these tools to claim and own your natural talents and abilities, and it will work for you.

Each leader can choose to expand their awareness and get out of mass density vibration levels at any time by:

1. Choosing to expand

2. Living in the question

3. Living in 10 second increments

4. Embracing ease, joy and glory

5. Letting go of form, structure and significance

6. Having no fixed point of view

7. Willingness to receive everything without judgment

8. Being in total allowance for everything

9. Trusting the flow of the universe.

Choosing to Expand

No matter who leaders are, nor what circumstances they find themselves in, their crucial choice is always the same—either to expand their awareness or contract it. Conscious leadership is the very process of expanding, not of arriving at a different set of limits. Conscious leaders are an unlimited being in this instant if they choose to be. Choosing to expand is completely internal. That is, it has nothing to do with anything or anyone else except leaders themselves. It is the commitment to themselves that they never let themselves live by anyone else's judgment and reality ever again, no matter what—not even their own judgment, whatever it takes. This, of course, works only if leaders are sincere and willing to be aware, and awareness is the key to consciousness.

When leaders choose to expand, they have to be willing to create a life that is greater than what they now have. The only way leaders can create in the moment and be on the edge of creation of their life is if they are willing to destroy everything they have decided is their true experience. Leaders have to be willing to be indefinable and willing to be receptive, yielding, open and naturally connected to life, spirit and all that is. When choosing to expand, leaders have to give up the idea that there's something wrong with them, and they have to give up all the "I am's......" Definition is always limitation. The essential questions that leaders have to consider are *"Am I willing to give up everything I think I am or everything I've pretended I am? Am I willing to give up everything I've decided I am or I've decided I should be?"* If leaders will destroy and uncreate all those realities, they can receive everything that is available to them, and all new possibilities can show up in their lives. When leaders destroy and uncreate everything they have decided their experiences are, they will open the door to constantly be in the state of creation of their lives rather than living it based on the past. In this state of creation of their lives, when leaders are truly being, truly connected and allowing the grace of life to flow through them, they are experiencing expansion.

Choosing to expand entails opening our heart, being in the moment, choosing with awareness, and having a willingness to experience our existence without form, structure and significance. If leaders are choosing anything other than joy, bliss, ecstasy, happiness, abundance, etc, they are functioning as unconsciousness. The basis of choosing to expand is to ask this question, ***"What am I choosing here in this moment—expansion or contraction?"*** There is incredible power in the simple declaration ***"I choose to expand. I choose ease, joy and*** *glory"* Ease, joy and glory are the energy and the manifestation of leaders' knowing. True knowing is the ultimate freedom.

> *The only thing that gives true freedom is knowing,*
> *and the only thing that gives true knowing is total consciousness.*

Another great question to use regularly is *"How does it get any better than this?"* (Don't try to answer this; let the universe answer it for you.) Asking this question is one of the fastest ways to lighten the energy of a situation. It is the ticket for getting out of where leaders are stuck. If leaders find themselves having some kind of difficulty or are involved in an incongruity, or even if they are feeling agitated, weary or out of sorts, the best way to lighten the energy is to ask the question, *"How does it get any better than this?"* When leaders use this question, they are inviting the universe to provide them with information, to tell them or show them how it gets better. What's more, if leaders are in a situation in which things are working out well, or they are feeling great, leaders can also ask "How does it get any better than this?" This is a powerful question to ask, as it invites the universe to show leaders that there are infinite possibilities. If the energy is light and ease, it will get even more glorious and magnificent. So, whether something goes wrong in a leaders' life or whether something goes right in their life, just keep asking, *"How does it get any better than this?"* as an invitation.

Key Points

- Recognize that your thoughts, feelings and emotions are only energy; they have no significance unless you make it so. If you make it significant, you make it heavy. If it is significant, it becomes solidity and then you have trapped yourself.

- Whenever you find yourself "doing the right thing" or behaving the right way, rather than the way that lights you up and feels more expansive, you are being unconscious and on the road to anti-conscious.

- Whenever you find yourself doing discrimination, judgment, differentiation, rejection, expectation, and separation, you are choosing contraction.

Living in the Question

A tool for leaders to really begin to create their lives and their realities with awareness is to live in the question. Living in the question is a most powerful tool from Access Consciousness that enables us to function from the knowing, as it can facilitate leaders to perceive outside a fixed and limited view of reality, beyond the limited and illusive content of thought. When conscious leaders learn to live in the question rather than being besieged by the problems or become vested in finding answers and solutions, they are able to create their life more consciously. By living in the question, conscious leaders are able to be totally present, able to function in the simultaneity of past, present and future and thus not be influenced unconsciously by past events or future concerns.

Most people function as if they are living in some kind of a maze and are desperately looking to find their way out. They create their lives and their realities by trying to know the answers to who, what, when, where and why they are, and always try to create a clear picture from the illusive content of their mind. These people create their lives by directing statements or are delivering vested answers at the universe, or towards themselves and others, rather than asking questions. Their statements, vested answers and inner messages accumulate at various levels of leaders' consciousness. Some are deeply embedded and insidious and many are disempowering, which limits leaders' perceiving, knowing, being and receiving. To create their reality consciously, leaders need to stop stating what it is, and start living from the question. When leaders are stating and defining the problem, they are operating out of finiteness, not infiniteness—this keeps them in the box with no way out. Any time leaders vest themselves in the problems or the answers, they have given it form, structure and significance. This can take a leader's freedom away without them realizing it. Learning to be conscious of what they are thinking and stating to themselves and others is very important, catching themselves being conscious of what they are thinking and stating is the key.

To become conscious of what they are thinking and stating to themselves and others, leaders may want to take a few moments to reflect on what statements guide them through their day. What do they think or state to themselves when they awaken in the morning? ......When they get ready for work? ....When they meet with a client? .... When they prepare for an important meeting? ....When they make decisions affecting other people? ....When people come to them with their problems? ....When they are in the work environment? ....When they are spending time with their friends and family? .... When they fall asleep at night? As leaders become aware of their normal and habitual statements or questions, leaders may find that the statements are helpful or unhelpful; empowering or disempowering; clear or confusing. Some may lead leaders to the responses or answers that they truly desire; some may evade the true issues.

The statements leaders use in their mind can have a major bearing on their lives.

Leaders' lives are created by the choice of the statements they are thinking and using in this moment. If leaders are not happy and content with the way their lives are happening, leaders need to look at the thoughts they are having. If leaders want to change their experience, they need to destroy and uncreate their current thinking in order to perceive something new. Leaders need to cultivate the attitude of inviting curiosity, of willingness to give up the need for being right, in order to allow the new possibilities to manifest in their life. The key is to be conscious and aware of the quality of their thinking. Whenever leaders perceive themselves having negative and unproductive thoughts, or being besieged by problems, or vested in finding answers and solutions, leaders can choose to replace them with more conscious questions. Living in the question is a process that allows leaders to gain access to pure consciousness and infinite possibilities. Questions are powerful magic. A question empowers, whereas an answer most often disempowers and limits. Asking questions allows the answer to manifest by allowing the universe to provide clarity. The universe has all kinds of unlimited answers that leaders don't have available to them because they try to function from their finite point of view of *"I've got to figure it out."* When conscious leaders live in the question, rather than trying to figure the answer out, they allow the universe to provide an answer which is greater than leaders can determine or imagine.

> *The Universe is an unlimited place with unlimited possibilities; it will give unlimited answers if leaders choose to ask questions.*

Living in the question allows conscious leaders to bypass their mental control, and remove judgment, rationalization and justification. Mental control and linear thinking impair the leaders' clarity and prevents them from perceiving what is possible beyond their limited imagination or expectations. When leaders ask the question, things start to show up in magical ways. By asking questions, leaders allow the universe and their inner knowing the opportunity to provide answers that the mind cannot figure out. However, if leaders say the answer is "..........." instead of asking the question, they will instantly limit the possibilities and stop the unlimited answers from manifesting. The certainty is that if leaders are able to function in the question instead of searching for the answer or focusing on the problem, their lives and circumstances will become ease, joy and glory.

Here are examples of what people often say to themselves when they deal with business issues and concerns: *"This is so complicated I don't event know where to start. I can't get my head around the details.....!! I don't know how to deal with this situation....!! My job is on the line if I can't fix this problem. I've got to figure it out....!! I don't know what to do about this problem....!! I am so worried; I can't possibly do this....!! etc."* If leaders think *"I can't do this,"* are they ever going to be able to do it? Instead of having these unproductive thoughts and being overwhelmed by problems, leaders can choose to ask the more conscious questions such as *"What is it I'm not getting about this? What am I pretending not to know or denying I know about this....? What would it take for....this to happen? What are the infinite possibilities that this will work out much better than we could ever imagine?"* These questions are exceptional tools for how to know what is the appropriate thing to do about the situation or the problem. When leaders ask these types of questions, things start to show up for them in a different way. The more leaders ask the question, the more aware leaders become of the options and possibilities they have. When asking the question, it is essential to avoid having expected outcomes. The key question is, *"What are the infinite possibilities in this moment?"* In this way, unlimited potential and infinite possibilities will emerge in ways that leaders may never have imagined possible.

The questions must be asked with genuine wonder, not with attitude and certain expected outcomes. Stop seeking answers; instead put the focus on the questions themselves. The magic is this: if leaders ask the questions with total awareness and with sincerity and from their heart, their life itself will become a living answer to them. Transformation can happen through sincere questioning, because leaders shift from the zone of lack and limitation and scarcity to the zone of infinite possibilities. If leaders ask the question in a non linear and unlimited way, and if they don't have a preconceived idea and expected outcome about the answer, they set the stage for previously unthinkable leaps of consciousness. If leaders open up to genuine wonder, they step out of the zone of this reality and into that of infinite possibilities.

Example of Questions for Use in Everyday Life

- What is it going to take to get this or to create this or to have this?

- What is it going to take for this to happen?

- Would an infinite being choose this?

- What is it that I won't allow myself to have that will give me the most expansion?

- Which way do I go to get the most expansion possible in my life?

- How can I facilitate the increase of oneness by doing ....?

- What is it going to take to make this....a total success?

φ φ φ

Living in the Question at Work and in the Business

One of the most important skills in business is to make accurate and expansive business decisions. However, most leaders tend to be tentative and cautious about making business decisions due to fear of making an incorrect choice. Unconscious leaders tend to think that *"It is hard enough to make a decision, let alone always make the correct ones."* In contrast, conscious leaders expound the virtue of using their intuitive knowing to guide them towards making the most expansive decisions. Conscious leaders are in touch with their intuitive knowing as well as the logical aspect of themselves. They are very skillful at combining their intuitive knowing with all the information they have on business matters and make their decision accordingly. From our own experience, accurate and expansive business decisions always engage leaders' abilities to perceive, know, be and receive. In others words, does it sound right, does it add up right, does the energy feel right, and is it expansive for everyone concerned. These factors must be used in unison when leaders make business decisions. Leaders must be aware that the choices or the results that come to them will seldom seem rational and logical at first. However, leaders must cultivate a self-assured trust in their knowing to make expansive decisions through clarity of asking questions that will augment the flow of the correct choices. Leaders must become aware of and receptive to the flow of expansive choices, which often comes in the form of new and further questions.

Harnessing an intuitive knowing for business decision making is of the essence for conscious leaders. The reality is that if leaders live in the question instead of the answer, they would be able to always function from their knowing. Learning how to ask the right question is the most important thing that leaders can become skilled at. The best questions leaders can ask are *"What would it take for me to ask the right questions for this business to happen?"* or *"What would it take for me to ask the right questions for me to make a correct decision,"* or *"What would it take for me to ask the right questions to get this…accomplished?"*

The question must be asked sincerely from a place of wonder instead of justification. When conscious leaders function from their intuitive knowing, they are able to perceive solutions that cannot be worried out by the clear light of logic. Conscious leaders look at situations from the framework of wanting to get to the truth. Asking these questions in the decision making process creates a pinnacle view, an expansive awareness view, which is the foundation for strategic decision making, enhanced creativity, and will bring out the best in people.

> **The reality is that if we live in the question instead of the answer our lives will become ease, joy and glory.**
> —G. D., Access Consciousness

Operating the business with questions can open up to possibilities of new ways of doing, working and functioning. There are substantial values lost in organisations when leaders do not ask simple questions. Such questions probe the essential details, cut through the hot air, clarify the nonsense, wipe out the drivel, and shed light on hidden meaning. Asking employees questions will often lead to a new perspective that leaders might not have envisioned and this will also empower the employees to know that they know. Asking the right questions is an indispensable skill for leaders and is linked to the skill of perceiving, knowing, receiving, hearing and detecting what is said and what is not said. Asking questions in business meetings allows people to know that they know and allows them to tap into their knowing. By asking and following the energy, leaders will be able to know what question to ask next and to know what people can and can't receive. By noticing the energy that led to the question, leaders will be led to the awareness of where the person sits. When leaders ask enough questions, they will get to that place. By noticing the energy, leaders will be able to recognise when they know something. They start to hear differently. Leaders will be able to hear the words of limitation coming out of the person's mouth. Things that are limiting the person the most will come right out of their mouth every time. If leaders are able to follow the energy and the impact it has on their awareness and thoughts, it is far easier to identify the issues and ask the question that brings forth useful and truthful information.

When leaders follow the energy, they can instantly perceive and know whether the information is truthful, untruthful or has been filtered in some way. Truth always makes leaders feel lighter. If something makes leaders feel heavy, it's untruthful or it has been filtered in some way. If leaders think **truth** before they ask any question, the person by decree of the universe must tell the leader the truth, and if they don't tell the truth, leaders will know that the person is lying or filtering the information.

Living in the 10 Second Increment

Living in the 10 second increment is an Access Consciousness tool for living in the present moment. Most unconscious leaders function predominantly with their thoughts in the past or the future, not aware that they are missing the vast array of infinite opportunities which always exist in the present moment, in this 10 second increment. On the other hand, conscious leaders know that their power is always available in this present moment, in this 10 second increment in time. When conscious leaders live and function in the 10 second increment, they know what is important for them, and they act on that knowing. They become the conscious navigator of their own reality. Conscious leaders claim, own and acknowledge the ability to perceive everything in the universe and relate to life in spontaneous interaction with the energy of the moment. Conscious leaders live by their own awareness, consciousness and abilities, moment by moment. They are able to see the big picture and the smallest detail at once because they claimed, owned and acknowledged their ability to perceive, know, be and receive.

Conscious leaders know that they are in command of this 10 second increment in time, if they choose to exercise it.

A key ingredient in living in the 10 second increment is the willingness to let go of a fixed position and all of the pretended stability, safety, predictability and constancy. A fixed position is the limitation that keeps leaders from perceiving, knowing, being and receiving. Living in the 10 second increment also requires leaders to be willing to not function with past reference points and to live without projections and expectations of what the outcome should be if they choose such and such. Each time a leader refers to past reference points, they do not choose in the moment. Functioning from past reference points causes leaders to miss the vast array of infinite possibilities and opportunities which are available and accessible in each 10 second increment.

To fully live in the 10 second increment, leaders must be willing to trust that they are supported by the universe and that they will handle whatever comes their way, no matter what the outcome may be. Here is an example of a simple and effortless approach in living in the 10 second increment (G. D., Access Consciousness):

You have ten seconds to choose the rest of your life, what are you going to choose? All right, that life is over; you have ten seconds to choose the rest of your life, what are you going to choose? That's how it's done. We have to choose in ten second increments. If we are choosing anything other than joy, bliss, ecstasy, happiness, abundance, etc we're functioning at unconsciousness.

When conscious leaders focus their attention in 10 second increments at a time, they become aware and conscious during that moment. They are not functioning from obligation, projection, expectation, judgment or desire and just choose to do it consciously in the 10 second increment. They will not be experiencing an urge to do something else, to think about something else or to be somewhere else. Conscious leaders will be able to perceive, know, be and receive with the clarity that they have so many choices, and that they can function in greater consciousness, without linear cause and effect. If leaders create it in anything other than 10 second increments, they are creating from the projection and expectation of the future, which never arrives, or from the constraint and limitation of the past based on their past experience. To fully relate to life in spontaneous interaction with the energy of this 10 second increment, leaders would have to be willing to be open, vulnerable and curious about each new moment. When leaders live in the 10 second increment they actually open the door to constantly be in the state of creation of their lives rather than living it based on the past. Then leaders will be able to receive everything that is available to them, and all possibilities will show up.

The ultimate endeavor here is for leaders to be the one who chooses, not to be the effect of anything.

One of the indispensable tools for choosing consciously in the 10 second increment is "asking the question." When leaders ask the question before making a choice, they will shift away from automatic, repetitive cycles and toward more conscious awareness. When leaders are fully conscious, they will be able to make powerful, life enhancing choices. Asking these questions below will facilitate leaders to bypass their limiting emotional states. When leaders ask these questions, they can instantly perceive whether the choice they are about to make is expanding or contracting their intensity of consciousness. Leaders may perceive the reply to the questions in the form of "yes/no" or the perception of "light/heavy."

- What am I choosing in this 10 second increment?
- Would an infinite being choose this?
- Would this choice be expansive for me and everyone concerned?
- Would this choice empower me or disempower me?
- Would this choice lead to a creation of a conscious future or would it keep me trapped in the past?

Key Points

- When conscious leaders create their reality by asking questions in the 10 second increment, they are fully present, open and vulnerable. They follow their knowing and energy of the moment, trusting that they are doing what is appropriate for that moment.

- To fully live in the 10 second increment, leaders must be willing to trust that they are supported by the universe and that they will handle whatever comes their way, no matter what the outcome may be.

- It is essential to let go of expectation, projection and what you think should be happening; this will allow you to immerse yourself in what is actually happening.

Embracing Ease, Joy and Glory

What would it be like to have all of life come to you with ease, joy and glory?

Having a life of ease, joy and glory starts with embracing ease, joy and glory where leaders are, and beginning to acknowledge the magic that they create. *Glory* is an exuberant expression of life and abundance in all things. What is abundance in all things?—*"abundance in all things is the understanding and reality that we are connected to each and every being upon this plane, to each molecule upon this plane and that every one of them is in support of us and the energy and power that we are"* (G. D., Access Consciousness). If leaders function as anything less than that, they are just choosing to be lesser than whom they can possibly be. This insight is also confirmed by the findings of quantum physics. At the heart of quantum physics is the discovery that everything is connected, that things exist through their relationships. Every component of a system has the potential to affect all the other components. Leaders cannot move without influencing everything in their universe. Leaders cannot even observe anything without changing the object and themselves.

A key step in allowing all of life to come to leaders with ease, joy and glory is to celebrate themselves from where they are, and having a gratitude for the rightness of themselves in this moment. Gratitude is a way of celebrating the rightness of whatever is in leaders' life and creating more space for infinite possibilities to come their way. If leaders are not constantly expressing gratitude for what they have, they will stop that flow. Leaders should do anything and everything in their power to celebrate their uniqueness and increase their bliss and joyfulness. It is all choice. Leaders are unlimited beings, and as such, they have the power to create the reality they want, no matter how miserable a life they are currently living.

Leaders have created their world exactly as their thought patterns are. Rather than focusing all of their attention on the wrongness of them and their life, leaders should simply find ways to celebrate themselves. There is a tendency to go *"What's wrong with me?" "What's wrong with this?"* If leaders focus on what's wrong with them or what's wrong with their life, they contract their awareness and become limited. Instead, leaders can ask, *"What's right about me that I'm not getting?"* or *"What is it that I'm not getting about this?"* If leaders ask these questions, they will start to perceive and get the answer. The question *"What is it that I'm not getting about this?"* will allow leaders to see the rightness of things rather than the wrongness of things.

In order to have ease, joy and glory in their life, leaders must be willing to have **Ease, Joy and Glory** in their life. Leaders need to reflect on *"Are they willing to allow all of life to come to them with ease, joy and glory? Are they choosing to live their life from the point of view of celebration everyday? Are they willing to let go of trauma and drama?"* Ease, joy and glory is only a matter of choice. Ease, joy and glory are our birth right, however most people don't choose to have them because they are addicted to polarity, to trauma and drama. Does ease and joy and glory mean that you will have only good things happen? No. *"What it means is, no matter what happens, it will come with ease and joy and glory, so even that which is bad will not be terrible. Even that which you find difficult will be greater in ease. And so it is that you will shift and change your world"* (G. D., Access Consciousness). So, whenever leaders use *"All of life comes to me with ease, joy and glory"* they are setting in motion that all the good things and all the bad things will be easier and more joyful and glorious. All of the circumstances in leaders' lives will start to get easier, regardless of the leaders' consideration and assessment of them.

Creating life as a celebration starts with the willingness to claim, own and acknowledge that life is an abundance of everything; life is an abundance of joy, abundance of ease and abundance of possibilities.

The key to claiming, owning and acknowledging is to become aware of any area of a leaders life that they believe doesn't work the way they would like it to. This can include the *usual* stuff people often have challenges, trials and tribulations with, such as not being happy and joyful, not being willing to go for what they know they are capable of, relationship problems, financial problems, not enjoying their life, not feeling fulfilled in life, etc. Leaders can then use *"All of life comes to me with ease, joy and glory"* to facilitate the shifting of energy to allow the areas of their life that they are not delighted with to flow with ease, joy and glory. It can be helpful to apply this to work, relationships, family, health, sports, financial situations etc. This mantra can also help shift moods that leaders do not particularly like, by repeating it until the mood shifts. The mantra will release the attachment and energy of judgment that leaders have on the point of view, and free them from it and begin the process of allowing leaders to change their life. This is not the same as doing the traditional visualization or routine habitual affirmation practices. It is not about pretending to be something that leaders are not or attempting to reprogram their mind for creating things in the material world. What leaders are doing with this mantra *"All of life comes to me with ease, joy and glory"* is inviting the universe to provide them with exactly what they have asked for, which is a life of ease and joy and glory. If leaders take a few minutes a day to focus on this mantra, they can shift their consciousness. The mantra will facilitate leaders to become more aware of those areas of their life that they do have abundance with, but have not been willing to claim, own and acknowledge. When leaders are able to focus, they can access their knowing and power that they can have ease, joy and glory, and they can allow it to be present in their life.

Key Points

- Gratitude is a way of celebrating the rightness of whatever is in a leaders' life and creating more space for infinite possibilities to come their way.

- Creating life as a celebration starts with the willingness to claim, own and acknowledge that life is an abundance of everything; life is an abundance of joy, abundance of ease and abundance of possibilities.

- By using the Access mantra of *"All of life comes to me with ease, joy and glory,"* leaders are indicating to the universe that they aspire to have all of life come to them with ease and joy and glory.

Letting Go of Form, Structure, and Significance

Form, structure and significance are the default map, the control system and the repetitive and automatic programming that most unconscious and anti-conscious people function from. They have a fixed and limited view of reality based on past reference points or future projections and expectations. Traditional organizational leadership tends to operate based on form, structure and significance since these leaders require a feeling of certainty and predictability which form and structure provides. They make this significant when this form and structure is not available. Conscious leadership, on the other hand, is inclined to thrive on uncertainty, without form, structure and significance. The key difference between traditional leaders and conscious leaders is that traditional leaders will seek to establish limits, whereas conscious leaders will look beyond them. Form, structure and significance creates commitments, infinite limitations, liabilities and obligations in leaders' lives. It allows no choice. It keeps life at arms length, and if leaders continue to live and function based on form, structure and significance, they will never be able to express themselves to the fullest.

What would it be like to live life from a sense of adventure and not from having a default map?

For leaders to expand their awareness and get out of mass density vibration levels, it is vital to let go of all form, structure and significance and to be in a constant state of creating themselves new, moment to moment, instead of maintaining their identity. What this means is to no longer live by the rules of this reality, but to live at the creative edge of this reality, to be open to life in such a way that celebration becomes their natural state of being. No form, no structure and no significance allows leaders to see life as an extraordinary adventure, to experience life in a serendipitous state and to create themselves new in every moment. It is about being indefinable, and not creating their life based on identity, definition or past reference points. Every identity and definition is a limitation, anything leaders value most in this reality becomes a trap which is a limitation for them. When leaders create from an identity, they create from a limited point of view, since each identity is a limitation of the infinite beingness that is the truth of us.

Limitation Is Self-imposed

Many leaders who follow the traditional leadership paradigm are convinced that they must have form and structure to ensure the business is focused on doing things in a consistent and predictable manner throughout the organisation. This form and structure becomes totally significant when large parts of the work processes and procedures are created just to keep this form and structure in place. These leaders become more concerned about the form and structure being the only right way of doing things; they allow it to rule over them and the organisation. They make form and structure greater than them. When form and structure becomes so significant in the organisation, it ensnares leaders to a belief that their way is the only way, and they concentrate all their energy on proving that they are right. The mere fact that these leaders believe in the concept of a *right way* is an expression of their limited perspective. On the contrary, conscious leaders recognise that there is no right way and no wrong way—just ways, just different points of view.

Leaders hold themselves captive by what they have made significant in their life. Whatever leaders give form, structure, and significance to, owns them. When leaders make anything of significance, they allow it to have power over them. No form, no structure and no significance allows leaders to see life as an exciting adventure that they can explore enthusiastically and deeply. To function in the present moment, leaders must choose to let go of form, structure and significance and aim to function as if the past never existed and the future is not pertinent. Each morning leaders can choose to say to themselves *"Who am I today and what grand and glorious adventure will I be having on this day"* This is a great way to consciously start the day.

Form, structure and significance drives leaders' thoughts and beliefs and most importantly "their choice," which most often is not a choice, but hidden forces that shape their realities. Unconscious leaders who function based on form, structure and significance tend to have fixed rules and unrealistic expectations. They regularly use the word *should, ought, must,* and *can't.* This leads to unnecessary frustration and disappointment. When leaders operate their life from form, structure and significance, they can be certain that they are not present in the here and now. With form, structure and significance in place, leaders are linearizing their reality so they have no choice. They are looking to every negative reference point in their lives to determine what they do and don't do. It totally denies their knowing.

In general, unconscious or anti-conscious leaders function for the most part based on form, structure and significance in order to have predictability, stability, constancy and safety in their lives. Attachment to form, structure and significance is one of the most restricting obstacles that confront leaders as they aim to expand their intensity of infiniteness. It is the leaders' own withdrawal from awareness, their own mass condition which makes them unable to totally function in perceiving, knowing, being and receiving. The most vital thing leaders can do is to become fully aware of the form and structure and significance that they have been conferring with. This will give leaders an idea about how they have been creating their lives. Without this awareness it's easy to fall prey to these issues and the manner they dictate leaders' habitual behaviors.

- How many reference points do you have to hold you back?
- What are the defined limitations of your life?
- To what extent are you and your business operating according to outmoded practices, policies and systems?
- How much form, structure and significance have you aligned and agreed with that stops you from expanding your awareness?

- What limiting beliefs do you function from in life that are creating your reality?

- How many systems and structures used in your life and your organisation exist because they have always been done that way?

Stop Making Anything Significant

When leaders make anything significant, in particular their thoughts, feelings and emotions, they have made it solidity; they allow it to have power over them. They make these thoughts, feelings and emotions greater than them. All thoughts, feelings and emotions are only energy; they have no real significance unless leaders make it so. It is essential to keep the thoughts, feelings and emotions as energy flow. Leaders can create the energy flow by asking the question *"What am I making significant here?"* What is the value of holding on to it?

Anything that we make significant, anything that we perceive greater than us, limits us. When we buy the significance of our thoughts, feelings, emotions, when we buy the significance of our point of view, when we buy the significance of other people's points of view; each and every one of those creates reality and limitation. What it amounts to is that every time we make anything significant, we are buying and functioning from a mistaken belief and misapprehension. These prevent us from ever being able to be truly free in that area of our life.

To let go of form, structure and significance, leaders can choose to apply the Access Consciousness tool of *Lightness* to anything they make significant. This will facilitate a shift of energy and a change in their consciousness and everybody around them. Every time leaders feel the energy of some consideration, idea, belief, decision or attitude becoming either significant, urgent, or imperative, they can feel where it hits them in their bodies. Feel the weight of it and turn it to light, and see it as only an interesting point of view.

Key Points

- When leaders have form, structure and significance judging that something is correct and right—then there is no room for something else to show up.

- To allow new possibilities to show up, leaders must destroy and uncreate what they currently have which they believe is right.

- Destroy and uncreate the relationship with everyone you have been in contact with everyday, so you can create your life new everyday.

- Magic happens when you stop being vested in the outcome.

- Willingness to step off the edge without prior knowledge of what is underneath it, is the true freedom.

No Fixed Point of View

To be conscious is to be in a state of flexible awareness, an open mind. This state can be brought about by claiming and owning the freedom to have no fixed point of view about anything. Every point of view that leaders have created about anything creates the limitations and parameters from which they receive it. Cultivating a frame of mind of *no fixed point of view* will allow leaders to perceive beyond a fixed and limited view of reality, knowing outside the content of thought, and receiving the unlimited infinite possibility of experience.

Unconscious leaders who function based on a *fixed point of view* are conformist and predictable. These leaders have fixed ideas and quite often they don't know that they can change their point of view. Unconscious leaders with a fixed point of view often say phrases such as, "Oh no, that's not the way it is," and they often focus their attention on the "why something can't be done." The regularity of the refrains: "you can't do that," and "this is not the way we do things around here" is indicative of unconscious leaders operating with a fixed point of view. Fixed point of view boxes leaders in and limits their potential. It limits how much they can receive. If leaders have a fixed point of view on anything, they automatically deny the infinite possibilities that there are better and more expansive things available. With a fixed point of view, leaders can't see anything that doesn't match their point of view. When opportunities present themselves in the ways that do not match their view, leaders are not be able to perceive and receive it and often work against it or keep away from it totally. Once leaders have a fixed point of view, they then have created a box to self limit what is possible, and they and others have to align and agree, or resist and react. Therein lies much stress and misunderstanding.

A fixed point of view often spawns the *right* vs. *wrong* paradigm, which creates separation and divides the organisation and the people within it. A fixed point of view often gives rise to a fixation with proving that leaders are right by confirming others to be wrong. Whenever leaders have an attachment to being right, they are usually inflicted with intolerance, antagonism and narrow-mindedness. Each time leaders identify with their point of view, they have to make it right and they automatically and unconsciously try to defend it against others. Holding on to a fixed point of view means that the majority of leaders' energy is spent defending this point of view. When leaders try to defend a point of view, they have no freedom. The moment leaders defend anything, they are no longer free to choose. Leaders with fixed points of view often feel defensive and limited, not wanting to take any kind of risk. The degree to which either the leaders or organisation are functioning from a fixed point of view is in direct proportion to their inability to innovate. Consequently, the organisation would be operating in a weak position and organisational accomplishments would be hindered.

When leaders are making unconscious choices, they can be certain that they are making choices based on their fixed points of view. Unknowingly, they turn their lives over to their anti-conscious viewpoint. For example, if leaders have a fixed point of view that "money is in short supply and there is not enough to go around," they may find it impossible to obtain prosperity and money. If leaders have a fixed point of view about business strategy and misidentify the strategy as being an operational initiative, a tool for competing with the competitors, they will not be able to perceive how the strategy can establish a creative edge that will bring greater value to the organisation.

Letting Go of the Fixed Point of View

There are two ways to approach the process of letting go of a fixed point of view, and they both lead to the same result: claiming and owning your natural ability to let go of any fixed point of view on the spot and allow the energy to release. The first way is by choosing to destroy and uncreate the fixed point view. The second way is to make it infinite.

The First Way—Choosing to Destroy and Uncreate

- Identifying your limiting belief and your fixed point of view is a critical first step.

- Once you've identified what your fixed points of view are, you need to catch yourself in the act of having those fixed points of view and recognize them for what they are. You can repeat to yourself *"Interesting point of view I have this point of view."* This mantra will take out the attachment energy you have on the point of view and free you from it.

- Having brought your fixed point of view into your awareness, you now can choose to let it go by destroying and uncreating all of the attachments you have on it. You can also affirm to yourself that "I am choosing to destroy and uncreate all of my fixed points of view (or my judgment) about _____."

The Second Way—Making It Infinite

Take whatever point of view you have about other people or situations and make it infinite. This can be done by first feeling the energy of this fixed point of view, now reverse it and have it going the other direction and expand it larger and keep expanding it to a size greater than the universe. When you make the point of view infinite, you are opening your consciousness and this enables the point of view to drop away all by itself. It is as though you are removing the lid from a pressure cooker. Magnify the point of view to infiniteness; it would appear like empty space, if it is a lie it disappears, if it is the truth it becomes more substantial.

Identifying your fixed point of view and your fixed point of view is

Key Points

- All points of view are just an interesting point of view. When you are willing to let go of a fixed point of view, things will show up.

- To let go of your fixed point of view you have to be willing to be wrong. It is important to let go of defending your point of view of the need to be right.

- When you get upset or angry over a certain issue, you can be sure that you have a fixed point of view about that circumstance. You can ask, "What fixed point of view am I making significant here?"

- Leaders who have fixed points of view usually react to situations in a way that is often predictable, habitual and automatic. Cultivating *no fixed point of view* allows the possibility of something even more expansive showing up in your life.

Willingness to Receive Everything without Judgment

To have everything, you have to be willing to receive everything,
willing to lose everything and willing to give up everything.
The first thing you need to give up is your limitation.

—G. D., Access Consciousness

Unlimited capacity to receive is the ability to have everything in life that conscious leaders fancy. In order to create any kind of limitation, leaders have to cut off their receiving. It is only what leaders have decided they cannot receive that can limit what they can have in life. Conscious leaders, who are willing to receive everything and willing to lose everything, develop their self confidence to see things through and to overcome the inevitable obstacles. When leaders practice willingness to receive everything, they enjoy and have the benefit of everything as it is. They have no need to alter or change anything. As leaders allow things to occur in their lives with no resistance, they will allow everything to come into their lives, which means they allow currency and money to come, they allow prosperity to come, they allow all of life to come to them with ease.

Whatever is not working in leaders' lives and in their organisations, there is always something they are unwilling to receive that would allow it to work. This is because whatever leaders have a judgment of, they will not be able to receive. Willingness to receive everything without judgment involves letting go of all resistance to any energy, to thoughts, feelings and emotions. It means to have no resistance, no rejection, no negation and no refusal of any concept or relationship. This means no judgment in their mind and willingness to be aware fully of anything possible. Judgment generates irregular fear that can induce a destructive, toxic and caustic state within leaders. When leaders generate judgment, they cannot perceive anything that doesn't match their judgment. The remedy for this is to be willing to receive everything, to experience life without mental resistance or judgment.

Imperturbability and freedom is the ultimate byproduct of a willingness to receive everything in life. This is the intrinsic state of being when leaders are not disturbed and cannot be troubled by anything that happens in their lives. It is necessary to recognise that *willingness to receive everything* does not mean leaders have to allow others to control them or have power over them. Leaders can still choose and keep going for what is appropriate for them in that 10 second increment without resistance. Every time leaders let go of the feeling of unwillingness to receive, they have more power with less exertion and greater emotional sovereignty and resilience. Consider this *"If you could receive from everybody without judgment or without any point of view- what would that be like?"*

To be free from anxiety, fear, hatred, competitiveness, and other emotional upheavals, it is essential to cultivate the quality of willingness to receive everything without judgment. Emotional upheaval and turmoil is the insidious consequence of unwillingness to receive anything that leaders have judged to be wrong, bad, harmful and unpleasant. Here are some examples of unconstructive situations, sentiments, viewpoints and things that may initiate unwillingness to receive for leaders:

- Not wanting to deal with the crisis
- Resisting having, being, or doing something
- Fretting about how things ought to be
- Predicting the future and mind reading
- Not wanting to make mistakes
- Overestimating the chances of failure and misfortune
- Things in leaders' life or business they don't like and want to change
- Being stuck with a problem and feeling fearful of the consequences

When leaders are not willing to receive, they can be certain that they are creating their reality based on their assumptions and implanted fears. The foremost archetypal implanted fear is the fear of the unknown and unfamiliar. It can severely hinder leaders' ability to perceive, know, be and receive. Unintentionally, leaders turn their lives over to their anti-conscious thoughts, feelings and emotions. When leaders encounter undesired events, if they judge them and are not willing to receive them, they will contract their awareness and they make the energy of the events or things solid and heavy. By judging and resisting them, leaders will make it significant and real and they will be stuck with them; it is what leaders cannot receive or look at, that gets them in trouble. Judgment creates resistance which allows no choice. However, if leaders can remain calm and be willing to receive the undesired event without resisting or reacting, and be in allowance of themselves for disliking it, they will keep expanding their awareness.

Resistance is a contraction of awareness; it prevents leaders from moving ahead in all areas of life, especially in the area of personal expansion and contentment. When leaders resist anything, they become dense and contracted. When leaders cannot receive, they will not be able to manage or deal with difficulties because they will not be aware of its presence. Whatever leaders are not willing to receive or perceive in their awareness, they will stumble over in their life. *For example, if leaders are unwilling to receive being judged by other people, they may become overly concerned with other people's points of view. Leaders may become overly concerned with what people think of them. Unwilling to receive the judgment is quite insidious. It's one of the main things that stops people from having, doing, and being what they want in life.*

Are you willing to receive any judgment with ease?
Are you willing to receive, no matter what judgment
may be directed at you?

A key step for cultivating the quality of willingness to receive everything without judgment is the willingness to claim and own the capacity to receive, even though leaders have no idea what that really means. A simple ingredient for being willing to receive everything is to stop resisting and reacting to any interaction of anything or anyone. When leaders catch themselves resisting and reacting, they can ask the question *"What am I unwilling to receive here?"*, *"What do I create meaningful for me that is stopping me from receiving?"*, *"What would it be like to receive from everybody without judgment or without any point of view?"*

Being in Total Allowance of Everything

Key Points

- Look at what you are not willing to receive in your life. What you are unwilling to receive will limit the amount you can have in your life.

- At the bottom of our problem is always something we are not willing to receive. If you are not happy and contented, look first at what you are unwilling to receive in your life. When your life is not working as well as you would like it, there is always something you are not willing to receive.

- To have everything, you must be willing to give up everything, you must be willing to lose everything.

- How many judgments do you put in place to stop you from being able to receive everything and from doing something?

Being in Total Allowance of Everything

Total allowance is an endeavor that is available to all leaders all the time. Total allowance is about not aligning and agreeing, or resisting and reacting, to any point of view, including the leaders' own points of view. Aligning and agreeing is the positive polarity and resisting and reacting is the negative polarity. All of these are polarized points of view and none of them are allowance. A positive point of view is as limiting as a negative point of view, if not more so. If leaders are not willing to receive and perceive all energies as only interesting points of view, then they are doing alignment and agreement or resistance and reaction, which creates polarization. Polarized points of view cause leaders to withdraw from full consciousness. The more leaders withdraw from consciousness, the more mass-obsessed leaders become, the more solid, finite and limited the world becomes for them.

> **There is no freedom in polarity,**
> **there is only freedom in interesting points of view.**

'Allowance' will help leaders to free themselves from their limited patterns of behaviour, judgment, emotions, thoughts and feelings. Being in allowance of all things will allow leaders to rise above their present consciousness level. When leaders are being the infinite allowance they truly have and are, nothing will ever bother them. They will never be able to be upset again. Allowance is *everything is just an interesting point of view and our own thoughts are also only interesting points of view.* Being in total allowance means every time leaders meet head-on with a strong point of view they can choose to say, "Ah, interesting point of view," and be in allowance of it and don't make it reality. Each time leaders adopt being in allowance of whatever accosts them, they have shifted the consciousness of the world because they have not bought it, they have not resisted it, they have not reacted to it, and they have not made it reality. They have allowed reality to shift and change.

It is fundamental to recognize that every opinion or point of view leaders have about anything or any one that leaders believe to be correct and perfect, will stop other things from coming into their life. Everything leaders judged right or wrong, good or bad becomes a limitation of who they can really be. Every time leaders create their own thoughts as solid, they have created a limitation on themselves. It limits how much leaders can receive. Whenever leaders catch themselves making judgments or having "inane drivel" thoughts or fixed points of view about anything, just repeat to themselves *"that's an interesting point of view,"* or *"interesting point of view I have this point of view."* This statement will release the attachment energy that leaders have on the point of view and free them from it. If leaders would like to be freed from all of their unwanted patterns of behaviour, thoughts and feelings they can repeat *"interesting point of view I have this point of view"* for every point of view they have. If leaders can learn to live from an interesting point of view, then they will start to get out of trauma, drama, upset and intrigue.

It isn't what we or others do or say which disturbs our emotions or feelings and destroys our ability to maintain our inner peace. It is our judgment of us and others which causes emotional upheaval such as anger, guilt, anxiety, irritation and resentment. The only way to prevent anger, resentment, hatred or guilt from occurring in a leaders' life is to let go of judgment and be in total allowance of themselves and others. This can be achieved by choosing to be in total allowance of absolutely everything that leaders see in their minds, in their bodies, in their environment, in circumstances and in other people. See everything as an interesting point of view. *"Everything is just an interesting point of view,"* or *"What am I making significant here?"* When leaders are willing to be in total allowance, everything is just an interesting point of view, even all the annoyance, disturbance and tragedy. When everything is just an interesting point of view, leaders start to create choice. Leaders don't have choice otherwise.

When leaders are in allowance, they will be able to observe what is going on with other people. Every time leaders are being in allowance, they are able to perceive that the other person is sitting in their own quandary and dilemma, and don't have to be in reaction to it. Leaders can be in total allowance of the person. When leaders are able to be in allowance of others, they are able to maintain their inner peace. There is absolutely nothing to be achieved by disturbing our inner peace just because somebody does or says something which we don't approve of. To do so is permitting them to control and have power over us. As leaders master being in total allowance, they will be able to see everything as just an interesting point of view, which will free them from all sorts of conflicts.

Key Points

- Just stop buying the others' points of view—life is a choice.

- If leaders don't do interesting point of view, they do alignment and agreement or resistance and reaction with a point of view, which locks them up.

- If leaders learn to live as an interesting point of view, they will get out of trauma, drama, upset and suffering.

- The more leaders are able to maintain *"it is just an interesting point of view"* for every point of view, the more leaders are able to receive new opportunities and infinite possibility.

Trust the Flow of the Universe

Trusting in the flow of the universe is the process of recognizing that the universe is an infinite place that has no boundaries or limitations, and leaders can ask the consciousness of the universe to support them to expand their awareness and assist them to create the life that they choose for them. When leaders are able to trust in the flow of the universe, they can perceive *abundance in all things* within the universe. They invite all of life to come to them with ease, joy and glory. Leaders can start the process by using the mantra of Access, *"I allow the abundant universe to provide me with a multiplicity of opportunities, all designed to encompass and support my growth, my awareness and my joyful expression of life."* to facilitate shifting of the energy to allow the universe the opportunity to show us information that our minds cannot figure out. What you are doing with this Access mantra is inviting the universe to support you to expand your awareness and assist you to create your life with conscious awareness.

The key for trusting in the flow of the universe is to choose to relate to life in spontaneous interaction with the energy of the moment and claim and own the ability to perceive, know, be and receive everything. Quantum physics has discovered that the essential nature of the universe is the movement of energy and information, there is nothing other than energy and information and that all things exist through their communion and interaction. Conscious leaders create their lives consciously by following the energy and by consciously asking questions of the universe and then making conscious choices moment to moment based on the information and awareness they perceive. Examples of questions that conscious leaders often ask are:

- What is it going to take to get this or to create this or to have this?

- What is it going to take for this to happen?

- What are the infinite possibilities for.........?

- How does it get any better than this?

- How can I facilitate the increase of oneness (in everything that I do)?

Whenever there is any part of a leaders' life that isn't working the way they would like it to conscious leaders ask, ***"How did I create this?"*** By asking this question, leaders ask the universe to let them know exactly where they chose to deny that they know. Only through choosing to be unconscious do they create difficulties in their life. If leaders are truly being conscious, difficulties do not arise.

When conscious leaders allow themselves to trust in the flow of the universe, they are empowered to know that they know, as they are able to connect with their inner source. They are not attached to convention and are always willing to take risks and destroy and uncreate old systems, structures and routines for more expansive ones. It is fundamental to recognize that energy and information exist everywhere in nature. Instead of saying, "Something is terribly wrong" and judging it and themselves, ask, ***"What is this energy?"*** or ***"What do I know that I am pretending not to know or denying that I know about.........?"***

Key Points

- Conscious leaders are not attached to convention and are always willing to take risks and destroy and uncreate old systems, structures and routines for more expansive ones.

- To follow the energy you must give up control. When you are controlling you are not present.

- The key to trusting in the flow of the universe is to choose to relate to life in spontaneous interaction with the energy of the moment and claim and own the ability to perceive, know, be and receive everything.

~ 7 ~

Conscious Leadership and Organisational Effectiveness

"Consciousness" is at the core of both personal and organisational growth and expansiveness.

All leaders have the power to make an incredible difference. It can be a magnificent, affirmative contribution, particularly when approached with dedication to conscious awareness, or it can be a contracted contribution when it is approached with unconscious or anti-conscious thoughts, feelings and behaviors that contain unrecognized and unresolved personal concerns. Unsuccessful organizations are contracted not because of the dismal circumstances they are in; they are in dismal circumstances because their leaders are either unconscious or anti-conscious.

"Consciousness" is at the core of both personal and organisational growth and expansiveness. To expand consciousness, organisations need to have conscious leaders who are able to establish infrastructure that encourages growth of consciousness potential in individuals and groups that will provide exceptional benefits to both. Conscious leadership is the key to creating a balanced integration of organisation vision, strategy, operational realities and a culture of consciousness. A truly conscious organisation chooses to embrace a culture of consciousness and aims to operate consciously across the broad spectrum of the business concerns—from strategic planning, to recruiting, to operating systems and processes, to developing the vision that guides the organisation. The culture of an organisation powerfully shapes the identity and behavioral norms for the employees and stakeholders. It influences the employee's enthusiasm and impetus. The culture of an organisation can be either expanding energy or sapping energy, depending on whether it is conscious, unconscious or anti-conscious.

Leaders have a number of key responsibilities that can provide expansiveness to their organisation and people if chosen to be applied consciously.

- **Vision and strategy:** Conscious leaders create and articulate vision and strategy, which can provide the cohesion that enables all people to, at the very least, understand why they are doing what they do. Conscious leaders share this information freely and articulate the vision of the organisation to those who have an interest in the organisation.

- **Accountability:** Conscious leaders embrace accountability and transparency internally and externally, and embrace the notion of "here is what we said we would do, and here is what we did."

- **Change management**: Conscious leaders perceive change as expansive, enjoyable and a natural extension of vision and strategy. They assist staff and stakeholders to embrace infinite possibilities and to function in a state of creative expansion.

- **Risk:** Conscious leaders recognise risk as opportunity, and show their people that risk is exciting and full of potential for growth and expansion, rather than traumatic and to be avoided and protected against.

Responsibility 1: Vision and Strategy

The conscious leader is the custodian of the values and vision of the organisation, and as such uses these as a major filter or guidepost for decision making, resource allocation, accountability and communication, and to increase awareness of others about the reason for being of the organisation. Many leaders do not know what the vision is, or can rote repeat the words with no awareness or perception of the energy and intent behind the vision. The conscious leader taps into the energy and intent of the vision statement, and empowers people to assist in the expansiveness of themselves and the organisation through striving to achieve the vision.

Often the vision and mission statement are created through tortuous form and structure processes that create the energy of "Wow, glad that's over, but what does it mean?" There are numerous explanations and definitions of what is a "true" vision and "true" mission statement, which are inevitably misleading by placing too much significance on the form and structure, on whether something is part of the vision, or of the mission. It doesn't matter!! The conscious leader looks at the vision and/or mission statement, and asks the question "What are the key intents behind this?" These key intents are the manifestation of the energy created by the founders or the crafters of the statement. Even a poorly written or crafted vision/mission statement will still have elements of the original collective consciousness and energy that went into the creation of that statement. The conscious leader can identify this energy, and put words to it that embrace the "intent" or the energy behind the creation of such a statement. This is much more expansive than the rote learning of the exact words.

In conjunction with an awareness of the intent and energy behind the vision/mission of the organisation, the conscious leader views strategic planning as an opportunity to identify the top five or six things that the organisation (or Division or branch or department, depending on the organisational position the leader occupies) needs to achieve in the next two or three years in order to create an expansiveness for all concerned. By having these key things clearly defined and consciously communicated to the team, they will become more aware and mindful to not wander aimlessly or they won't settle for side steps that take them away from the true vision and mission of the organisation.

Strategic planning is often misidentified as being a bothersome operational initiative and misapplied as a process and subsequent document that is done because the CEO or Board want it done so that they can say they have one. Many is the time we have seen strategic plans that are either wish lists that are not measurable and that are reviewed annually, or are developed and written over a six month period, by which time everyone is tired of the "process," and want nothing more than to bury it.

The conscious leader regards the strategic plan as a guidepost for sharing information and vision, whilst remaining flexible based on relevant changes to the environment of the organisation and the world. The form, structure and significance of the strategic plan and the subsequent implementation that is found in so many organisations is supplanted by an awareness by the conscious leader, of the forces that impact on the organisation, and the monitoring and perceptive awareness of what is going on around the organisation. The more conscious rationale of the strategic plan is to establish a creative edge that will bring greater value and expansiveness for the organisation and everyone concerned.

The conscious strategic plan qualities are:

1. Engage the energies of the whole organisational network

2. Focus explicitly yet with no fixed point of view

3. Be aware, alert and open to infinite possibilities and new initiative

4. Embrace uncertainty whilst remaining focused on the core vision

The conscious leader ensures that the strategic plan is shared with all staff, and the vision/mission of the entity is used by all staff as the major filter for the programs of the organisation. The Board agenda, staff meeting agenda and staff reports all reflect the strategic plan, and the annual report utilizes the strategic plan as its main format for reporting to constituents. All staff are allocated to components of the strategic plan, and their job descriptions changed to reflect this impact. All staff have one or two Key Performance Indicators that reflect the key elements of the strategic plan as part of their performance system.

Conscious leaders also share information. They communicate the vision and values of the organisation through written and spoken words and symbols, and through the energy they create. Greater creativity, trust and openness is only unleashed when people perceive and receive the true vision and values of the organisation. Conscious leaders develop a common language to explain and link strategy with execution. They focus on trust, creativity, intuition, innovation, freedom, flexibility and generosity. They choose to create conditions for cohesion, community spirit, and mutual accountability. One of the fundamental impediments to successful strategic renewal is that many leaders tend to function unconsciously or anti-consciously about sharing information. These leaders tend to operate without open and clear communication lines; they often adopt a communication style that is rooted in the approach of smoke and mirrors.

Conscious leaders will continually ask themselves the following questions...

- What values are guiding my actions as a leader?

- What would it take for me to articulate a vision of the organisation when things are unpredictable?

- What are the infinite possibilities for me to improve my ability to inspire others toward a common purpose?

- What would it take for me to create an environment that promotes innovation and risk?

- What would it take for me to build a cohesive and spirited team?

- What would it take for me to share power and information and still maintain accountability?

- What would it take for me to put more joy and celebration into our efforts?

People listen to conscious leaders because they provide an energy that is sincere, truthful and resonates with the people listening.

Responsibility 2: Accountability

Leaders are given trust by the organisation and the people who follow them, and this trust is created through the leaders' accountability. This accountability is both external and internal to the organisation.

External accountability is shown by leaders through the way they communicate with shareholders, constituents, contractors, etc. The conscious leader knows that others take comfort when they know what the organisation had planned to do, and what it actually did, rather than how busy the organisation has been. This simple precept should be reflected in annual reports, where the organisation reports against what it said it would do (often the strategic or operational plan), and reports against achieving the vision of the organisation.

Internal accountability is created through evaluation processes for leaders and staff (simply put, this is what we agreed we should be doing, did we do it and how well did we and others view this). These evaluations should be crafted around how expansive the person is for other people and the organisation generally. Conscious leaders can develop evaluation systems that actually increase the awareness and consciousness of their people, and help them break out of any fixed points of view and judgments.

One form of accountability that is mostly misidentified and misapplied is the use of financial information as a measure. Money is only a measure of what you have planned to do versus what you actually did. Reading and analysing financial reports needs to be conscious and get away from the implant of money as the focus: the focus is on what is driving the organisation, which is measured, in some cases, by the use of dollars. The key to consciously using financial reports is to identify the underlying reasons why things are happening. For example, when using the Profit and Loss statement, look for the reason for variance, rather than focus on the figures. With the Balance sheet, look for the key ratios that tell you what the various relationships are. With the cashflow statement, look at the three month rolling cashflow so that if something is likely to happen, you know about it 2–3 months in advance, not after the event. Trust your intuition; if something doesn't feel right, or it feels "heavy," ask for clarification and reasons, and be aware of any unconscious filtering by you or by the authors of the information.

Responsibility 3: Change Management

Change management is often misidentified and misapplied as an issue of trauma, threat, stress and difficulty. Most people's apprehension and uneasiness to change is usually based on an implanted fear of the unknown and unfamiliar. This is an indication of how deeply attached these people are to existing form and structure, the comfort zone and the familiar way of being and doing. The conscious leader, however, perceives change as expansive, fun and a natural extension of vision and strategy. They recognize and trust change and are willing to envision that there are no limits to what they could create. Conscious leaders seek out and welcome change because they know that change is innate, inevitable and necessary for something else to be created. They build a culture of consciousness that embraces change and facilitates conscious change management.

Conscious change management is about empowering staff and stakeholders to embrace infinite possibilities and to function in a state of creative expansion that lets them go over their limits everyday, much more than they could ever imagine. Conscious change management advocates the view that the universe is one big matrix composed of infinite possibilities, and each individual leader, staff, stakeholder and business organization has a place in it. Conscious change management empowers people to perceive, know, be, receive and spontaneously discern phenomena from many different tangible and indefinable levels. It has been observed that when change management practices are not attuned to infinite possibilities, they are often implemented from a limited point of view and try to define everything according to a linear point of view. This is a solid physical mode, created in order to conform to long-established human perspectives. It is essential to recognize that most of the disturbances, suffering, distress and great effort which occur in unconscious and anti-conscious change management processes originate from their restricted ability to operate beyond parameters of finite and limited human perspectives. These traditional change management practices often antagonize staff or systems into changing and innovating, just as they might use fear as a motivator and point to its success. On the contrary, with a conscious change management perspective, these traditional methods are perceived as wholly inefficient and energy-draining strategies. With this point of view, structure, management and processes must be tailored accordingly in order to achieve the required alertness, responsiveness, velocity, creativity and resourcefulness to act profitably upon the new change prospect.

Conscious leaders claim and own their ability to perceive unlimited potential and inspire others with their vision of the new possibilities that are the byproduct of the change management course of action. When conscious leaders are attuned to infinite possibilities, they choose expansion, they become unlimited. They have a knowing that is not limited and not restricted in any way by time, space or physicality. They attune to that which has not yet manifested and let the infinite possibilities work for them. They empower staff and stakeholders to claim, own and acknowledge the ability to perceive everything in the universe and destroy everything that makes them think they have to solidify anything into perception. They encourage people to progress forward and to destroy the judgment of *change* as some kind of punishment. Conscious leaders choose to facilitate change in the organisation by living in the question, rather than trying to function from their finite point of view of "I've got to figure it out." They allow the universe to give them an answer, which is always greater than they could determine. The best questions leaders can ask are *"What would it take for me to ask the right questions for this change to happen with ease?*

What is it going to take for staff and stakeholders to perceive, know, be and receive change as a new opportunity for growth and improvement? What would it take for staff to see that there can be no improvement without change and no change without improvement?"

Conscious change management practices focus more on *transformation* than just *change*. There is a fundamental and critical difference between change and transformation. For example, if we freeze water, it will solidify and change to ice. However, if ice is placed in its usual environment, it will reverse back to water. Many traditional change initiatives have been like this water and ice example. Transformation, on the other hand, is the process of destroying and uncreating the old ways, even if they are perceived to be effective, so that new possibilities can show up. Transformation is when change creates an enduring and expansive difference.

If staff reaction to change is perceived as an issue, the conscious leader can assist staff to experience change as expansive by discussing the elements of change with staff very early in the process, rather than as an add-on or afterthought. Staff will tend to create their own erroneous reality when faced with rumors, non-sharing of information, or timorous and apprehensive behaviour from leaders. The conscious leader can provide some simple questions that may assist staff to break out of the unconscious or anti-conscious behaviors. These questions include:

- What judgments, projections and expectations do you have about the change that is causing you to be so fearful of the change?

- What is it that you are not getting about this?

- What is the value of holding on to this old form and structure?

- What have you misidentified and misapplied about this change?

- What are you unwilling to receive here?

- What are you making significant here?

- What awareness are you having here that you are not acknowledging?

- What is it going to take for you to let go of seeing the change as some kind of punishment?

By asking these questions, leaders will be able to perceive the transient illusive nature of thoughts, and break free of the energy that will otherwise limit the potential expansiveness of the change. The questions will provide a means for leaders to not focus on judgmental, destructive and limited thoughts. This process will allow higher order awareness, insight, and intuition to manifest spontaneously in themselves and staff.

Conscious organisations build a culture of consciousness that embraces change and facilitates conscious transformation initiatives with openness to new ideas and a sincere desire for positive and expansive transformation. The form, structure and significance of the traditional change practices and the enforced implementation that is found in so many organisations is superseded by empowering people to move beyond rigid mind-sets and learning to become more adaptable and flexible. The conscious transformation initiative qualities are:

1. Foster good open and clear communication lines that make the staff feel valued.

2. Willingness to receive all points of view by welcoming and hearing all perspectives.

3. Cultivate the environment that allows staff to recognize and trust change by developing the practice of making change as part of the everyday business functions.

4. Support staff to envision that there is no limit to what they could create by facilitating change constantly and encourage staff to discover more expansive and innovative ways of doing things.

5. Engage the power of caring to eliminate fear of change and instead embrace it with a sense of excitement and adventure.

Responsibility 4: Risk

Many people view risk as trauma and drama, something that needs to be protected against. The conscious leader views risk as an exciting opportunity to understand their business and people, and to grow and expand their opportunities. Risk is not inherently right or wrong, good or bad; it is more the things that happen outside our expectations that might have an impact on our ability to achieve the strategic initiatives of the organisation.

> *The winners of tomorrow will deal proactively with chaos,*
> *will look at the chaos per se as the source of market advantage,*
> *not as a problem to be gotten around.*

—Tom Peters

There are three types of risk that the conscious leader takes into consideration: Hazard, Uncertainty and Opportunity risk. Hazard risk includes physical risks such as fire and injury, asset risks such as non access to building, unsafe equipment, and environmental risks such as lack of controls on hazardous substances. Uncertainty risk includes financial risks such as foreign exchange, illegal use of funds and contract cancellation. Opportunity risk, often ignored, includes strategic risks such as misidentifying strategic initiatives because of fixed points of view and ignoring expansive opportunities, operating risks such as damage to reputation, and information risks such as inaccurate or filtered information. These risks are all opportunities just waiting for the conscious leader to perceive, know, be and receive the opportunity that has been presented to them.

Risk management is the conscious awareness of all the risks involved in the organisation, the strategic advantage of these risks, and the ease with which these risks can be managed. Though risk is inherent within all business opportunities, many leaders prefer to be risk averse. This can lead to missing opportunities. The very nature of business endeavors and success demands leaders to have a willingness to receive everything without judgment.

How risk is defined and acted upon is all a matter of choice of the leaders. Leaders can choose to view risk as bad, complex and to be avoided, or as a strategic advantage that can enable the organisation to undertake activities that others might not even consider.

Identifying risks involves the conscious leader not having a fixed point of view of what constitutes risk, and involving others who have different points of view about the organisation, and therefore different points of view about risk.

The conscious leader involves the board, senior staff, program managers, key stakeholders (e.g., financiers, clients, contractors, etc.) in ascertaining their points of view about risk facing the organisation. Once the risk has been identified, then the leader can ask the questions *"What can I do with this that would be expansive to my organisation and our people?", "What is it that I'm not getting about this?", "What are the infinite possibilities that this will work out much better that we could ever imagine?"* Shifting the focus to looking for the rightness of the situation instead of the wrongness of the situation, and doing what needs to be done, always changes adversity to a greater strategic advantage. It is very tempting for most people to say "How can I get rid of this risk," whereas it would be more expansive and strategically innovative to ask the question, *"This is exciting. What can I do with this risk that others would not consider, and what are the infinite possibilities that this opportunity can be expansive for us."*

~ 8 ~

The Value of Being a Conscious Leader

Conscious leaders have the capacity to perceive, know, be and receive the totality of life and the abundant business opportunities that benefit not just their organizations, but will affect all people who are impacted by those organization.

There are going to be some individuals who will read every word of this Conscious Leadership book and will still wonder, "So, what is the advantage of being a conscious leader and how would conscious leadership benefit the business?" This final chapter has been created to offer an insight and invitation into the value of being a conscious leader.

Conscious leaders are infinite beings who live in a constant state of creation of their lives in the moment. They are devoted to the expansion of awareness and the facilitation of consciousness in all things. They have power and capability to set in motion a conscious leadership spirit within a business context that engages both courage and know-how to break new ground and the bravado to go beyond limitations, narrow-mindedness and insularity. Conscious leaders have the capacity to perceive, know, be and receive the totality of life and the abundant business opportunities that benefit not just their organisation, but will affect all people who are impacted by that organisation, the entire workforce, the surrounding communities and the world at large. They consciously choose whatever they do or perceive, and they are able to function in the simultaneity of past, present and future without fixating on any one aspect of time. Conscious leaders create a balanced integration of organisation vision, strategic and operational realities by encouraging and nurturing higher levels of conscious behaviour and attitude among their staff and stakeholders. The degree to which conscious leadership exists within an organisation will be in direct proportion to the organisations growth and abundance.

Conscious leaders create the future for their organisation through their expression, their action, their presence and their way of being. They are living in a constant state of being connected and in communion with everything which enables them to receive everything. They perceive infinite possibilities and inspire others with their vision. They have the gift and the panache to articulate an extraordinary image of advantageous and beneficial opportunities and their beingness inspires people to follow their lead. Based on their ability to perceive, know, be and receive the energy, and by asking astute questions and observations of the business environment, global economic climate, client's behaviour and feedback, the marketplace, technology trends and scientific advancements, the conscious leader instigates new approaches, initiatives, products and solutions. The conscious leader guarantees the success of the business by following the energy that leads them to the next possibility, not the next limitation.

Conscious leaders advocate a new approach to elevate an organisation's way of being that is proactive and able to respond to challenge, emergency and change with equanimity, flexibility, coherence and balance. These attributes are essential today for an organisation to benefit from previously overlooked opportunities, as well as new opportunities; to attracting more business and for expanding market share. Conscious leaders are very vigilant about not having too rigid a form and structure. They will ensure that form is flexible and structure is not restrictive. They are fully aware that the organisation must build in flexibility just like the high-rise buildings in earth quake prone areas that are required to be built to withstanding changing foundations. The organisations that have an inflexible and unyielding 'form and structure' business arrangement and principles will not be able to move with agility and will ultimately fall in upon themselves.

Most businesses fail because of the fixed points of view that the leaders take. In todays swiftly evolving and increasingly changeable world, where performance requirements have increased rapidly, organisations cannot afford to deploy unconscious leaders who have a fixed point of view. A fixed point of view often generates professional complacency, squashed initiatives, promotes unconscious compliance and cultivates an unconscious organisation. Leaders with a fixed point of view facilitate an unconscious culture of fear and risk aversion. Unconscious leadership is strong on supervision but very poor at getting the best out of people and resources. This is because they have enshrined control through strict supervision, stipulated fixed points of view on procedures and processes, established inflexible rules and supported rigid reporting structures. This, in turn, produces inertia and great resistance to change. This illustration exemplifies the point that leadership can powerfully shape the identity and behavioral norms for the group. It can be an exceptional, affirmative behavior, when approached with conscious awareness, or it can be a contracted trait when it is approached with an unconscious or anti-conscious goal. The leaders' outlook and point of view strongly directs and persuades the choices the staff and stakeholders make, how they perform, how they feel and the way they interact with people inside and outside their organisation.

Conscious leadership is about facilitating expansion of consciousness and encouraging the spirit of others.

Conscious leaders are dedicated to awareness as a way of being in the world and to bring to each business activity a level of awareness appropriate to it. They develop close association with their staff, clients, suppliers and stakeholders based on gratitude, honor, trust, vulnerability, allowance, and showing respect and sensitivity. They follow the energy and are very adept at perceiving and reading the social dynamics of the team, handling disagreements diplomatically and consciously. They have an incredibly powerful position in influencing and shaping the attitude, mood, trait, and quality of their teams and their organisation. They develop leverage by enlisting the support and capabilities of others by making certain that the right interactions and communication are provided appropriately to all staff and stakeholders.

Conscious leaders facilitate staff and stakeholders to connect to heart and enthusiasm, and awaken the ability to perceive, know, be and receive. They build enthusiastic supporters and potent teams by listening to others, perceiving their requirements, receiving their requests, opening to the ideas of others and are willing to share power and accolades. The focus of conscious leaders is on always listening to even the least paid workers and recognizing when truth is spoken which leads to a constant state of ever expanding awareness and infinite possibilities of the joy of business. Conscious leaders are the creator of joy and possibilities. When conscious leaders embody their greatness they emanate an energy field of healing, nurturing, caring, creativity, aliveness, joyfulness, expansiveness and an intensity of infiniteness that allows all things to be possible.

~ 9 ~

Wrapping Up

Before we bring this book to a close, we would like to remind you that life is an abundance of everything. Life is an abundance of joy, an abundance of ease and an abundance of glory, it is the reality of the truth of you.

> *Know you as the greatness, Perceive you as the greatness*
> *Be you as the greatness and Receive you as the greatness*
> *Because that is the truth.*
>
> —G. D, Access Consciousness

If you are ready to live in this place, if you are ready for unbridled joy, an exuberant expression and abundance of life, regardless of life's challenges, all you have to do is choose to embrace consciousness and make consciousness the guiding principle in your life, your work and everything you do. Each time that you choose to expand consciousness, you change this world into a place in which people can truly live, with absolute awareness, absolute joy and absolute abundance. Not just you but every other being in this world is affected by the choice you make.

Background and About the Authors

This book is a gift to every individual, leader and organisation dedicated to creating a life that is greater than what they now have, and to making a difference in the world. The book is a creation of Chutisa Bowman, Steven Bowman and Gary Douglas based on a foundation of expanded consciousness and business experience that provides transformational tools that can unlock and open doors for leaders to be more conscious. This book empowers leaders to become conscious of and shift any part of their reality that isn't working. It shows leaders how to make the personal journey towards becoming powerful and conscious leaders. This book has been created to convey at a macro level the beingness and tools for all leaders and businesses endeavoring to become more conscious. The writing of this book has been a joyful and expansive experience and we trust that you will find something that relates to your own personal situation.

φ φ φ

Chutisa Bowman

Chutisa is a director and co-founder of "LifeMastery" based in Melbourne, Australia. She has embraced a career as an international advisor and facilitator in the field of transpersonal counseling, ergonomics, behavioral self management, and stress intervention. A former senior executive at a number of the Australia's largest publicly listed retail corporations and senior consultant with one of Australia's most prominent usability and human factors specialist consulting firms, Chutisa perceives and knows from first-hand experience what businesses and leaders need to do to become more effective and conscious. Concurrent with her ability in assisting individuals and organisations attain improved efficiency and wakefulness, Chutisa has insight into the challenges and opportunities in the integration of consciousness into a business environment. She has been focusing on developing processes to help companies build a culture of consciousness and conscious leadership teams, and helping people deal with everyday stress in demanding environments. Chutisa uses her own experience and many years of research to help today's leaders, managers and employees find balance to allow themselves, their workplace and company to expand their consciousness.

Trained as both a transpersonal and conventional psychophysical change facilitator, Chutisa received her undergraduate qualification from the IKON Institute in Transpersonal counseling, her postgraduate degree from La Trobe University in Ergonomics and Human Factors, and she is in the process of completing a Master degree in counseling at Monash University. Chutisa has gone beyond her traditional academic training, however, by acquiring depth and breadth of knowledge in a number of fields, including Access Consciousness, behavioral medicine, stress and well-being, HeartMath processes, meditation, consciousness, creativity and the great spiritual traditions of the world.

φ φ φ

Steven Bowman

Steven Bowman is a director and co-founder of "LifeMastery" based in Melbourne, Australia. Steve is sought after as an expert advisor to leading businesses worldwide on conscious leadership, strategic innovation and awakening the power of consciousness within organisations. Steve is one of Australia's leading Governance and Senior Executive Team specialists, having previously held positions as National Executive Director of the Australasian Institute of Banking and Finance, Chief Executive Officer of the Finance and Treasury Association, General Manager of ExpoHire (Australia) Pty. Ltd., Assistant Director of the Australian Society of CPAs, Director of the American College of Health Care Administrators, and Managing Director of Enterprise Care Not for Profit Services. He is a past President of the Australian Society of Association Executives, and has held numerous other Board positions. He has authored and co-authored over fourteen books on Governance and Executive Leadership. He was the founder and Associate Program Director of the Certificate and Advanced Certificate in Association Management at Monash Mt. Eliza Business School for eleven years. He and his partner Chutisa currently work with over 1,000 Not for Profit and corporate organisations each year in Australia, New Zealand and Asia in Governance, Executive Leadership and Consciousness at work.

Steve is a warm and engaging conference keynote speaker and dynamic workshop/seminar facilitator. He brings thirty years of hands-on experience and delivers it in a down-to-earth style that speaks to everyone throughout the organization. He leaves his audiences inspired with practical leadership tools and tips that to apply at work, at home, and in their communities.

Trained in both organisational management and as a behavioral scientist, Steve received his undergraduate degree in Applied Science: Speech Pathology from La Trobe University, where he also completed a post-graduate degree in Communication Disorders, and completed his Master degree from the George Washington University Washington D.C. in Speech Pathology where he also completed a Master of Association Management. He also earned a Certificate in Association

Management and Advanced Certificate in Association Management at
the Mt. Eliza Business School.

φ φ φ

Gary Douglas

Gary Douglas is a director and founder of "Access Consciousness"
based in Santa Barbara, California, U.S. Gary has extensive experience
in the business world. During his forty years in business he has expe-
rienced being director, manager, employer, entrepreneur, the leader of
organisations, a business owner, a consultant, a workshop facilitator
and a keynote speaker. Gary's career is vast; he developed, directed and
led a number of businesses, including real estate, restaurants, horse
training, and antiques prior to creating Access Consciousness. He has
worked with all types of organizations and people throughout the
United States, Europe, Asia, Australia and New Zealand, facilitating
and leading workshops empowering them to destroy all limitations
to creating exactly what they desire, and creating transformation in
their lives. Gary is a conscious leader in the field of consciousness and
energy transformation process. He is widely recognized as one of the
world's foremost catalysts in helping individuals to claim, own and
acknowledge their ability to perceive, know, be and receive and to
function as the infiniteness instead of the finiteness. His focus is always
on: "How do we get people to greater freedom, greater consciousness,
and greater awareness of their talents, abilities and capabilities?"

Gary uses his own methods to create his own dream job and life style.
He currently travels the world consulting with individuals and groups,
empowering individuals, leaders and organisations to become conscious and guiding them to personal freedom. A convivial, affable and
powerful presenter, Gary invites his listeners to empower their bodies,
hearts and psyches in the expansion of their consciousness.

More about LifeMastery

LifeMastery is an international practice dedicated to facilitating individual and organisational transformation through expansion of consciousness in the workplace so that consciousness can spread throughout society and transform the world. Steve and Chutisa have worked with presidents, CEO's, and senior leaders to bring about dramatic organizational improvements in a diverse range of industries, including health, trade, employment, financial, sports, telecommunications, religious, higher education, charity, philanthropic, welfare and community organisations. LifeMastery's capabilities and competence include aligning leadership teams and staff with organisational vision and strategies, creating synchronization and harmonisation amongst executives, leadership teams, staff and stakeholders, supporting CEO's and their teams to develop conscious and mindful partnerships with their Boards and designing conscious leadership development programs that achieve sustainable results.

LifeMastery is breaking new ground in therapeutic processes for leading organizational transformation. It provides a practical framework and comprehensive approach to help businesses expand and enhance their consciousness level, facilitating magnification of consciousness in governance and empowering directorships of Boards of commercial, public and Not for Profit organisations. Our personal dedication is one of inspiring individuals and organisations to expand their consciousness and to fulfill their potential. We perceive and live in the principle that the best way to achieve expansion of the world is through the facilitation of consciousness in all things.

LifeMastery has a proven track record of infusing leaders, teams and individuals with enthusiasm and excitement, focusing on creating a culture of consciousness in which people can find balance and become highly conscious, emphasizing not just professional and financial rewards, but also the psychological, emotional and intellectual rewards of a job well done.

For more information about LifeMastery and
Steven and Chutisa Bowman visit **nomorebusinessasusual.com**

More about Access Consciousness

Access Consciousness is an applied philosophy for living that has been successfully put into practice for expansion of life by individuals all over the world. Access empowers people to become conscious of, and shift any area of their lives that aren't working. This can include complexity with the common and everyday things people often have trouble and tribulations with, such as financial dilemmas, relationships, career obstacles, not receiving pleasure from life, not feeling satisfied or at ease in life, unsure of the purpose and impetus of life, not being blissful, not able to achieve what they detect they are capable of, etc. Access also deals with and brings clarity to some of the weirdest stuff people can experience. This can include hearing voices in your head, anxiety, depression, getting sick when other people around you are sick, and other physical problems. It works on just about anything and produces the possibility for a change in any aspect of life.

Access Consciousness assists individuals to embrace a place of infinite possibilities that reside within each of us. Access provides a set of tools and processes designed to create freedom from limitations of the past and enables people to create a life full of ease, joy and glory and constant wonderful surprises. Access tools and processes allow people to remove the limitations that shackle and chain them in life and shift what isn't working in their life and step into BEINGNESS and the MAGIC of Life!

Access is a gentle way to remove energy blockages and to unlock everything that does not allow people to be everything they would like to be, and to have everything they would like to have. Clearing these energy blockages allows the body, mind and spirit to align as Oneness. This creates dramatic changes in their interactions with others and in the productivity of their lives. Access began in 1990 based on information Gary Douglas channeled, and he has been developing and refining it ever since. Access uses both verbal clearing processes and simple but phenomenally powerful hands-on healing techniques to create increased consciousness. Most of the people who attended ACCESS workshops have discovered a new sense of what their potential is, how to unlock it, and how to access it. The techniques work on adults, children, and animals.

For more information about
Access Consciousness,
visit **www.accessconsciousness.com**

Scan for more information

Looking for a Speaker?

Are you interested in having one of the authors work with your organisation or your leadership team? Gary Douglas, Steven and Chutisa Bowman also provide on-site conscious leadership retreats and developmental programs for organisations, both domestically and internationally, on many subjects in addition to "Conscious Leadership."

Please check the websites for more details.

Steven and Chutisa Bowman
LifeMastery(Aust) PTY LTD
www.nomorebusinessasusual.com

Scan for more information

Gary Douglas
www.garymdouglas.com

Scan for more information

Also by
Steve and Chutisa Bowman

Leading from the Edge of Possibility:
No More Business as Usual

Just imagine what your business and your life would be like if you stopped functioning on autopilot and began to generate your business with strategic awareness and prosperity consciousness. This is truly possible, except you have to be willing to change. Recognizing a different possibility requires a different mindset and almost always demands a kind of awareness that is not part of prior experience. With this book you'll get the awareness you need to lead your business in any environment!

Prosperity Consciousness

You can know everything about investment schemes, financial strategies, real estate investment, and the top secrets of high finance. But if your awareness, or consciousness, concerning money is based on the scarcity paradigm, then you will never have the sense that you have enough money. Unless your prosperity consciousness expands, your relationship with money will remain unchanged.

CPSIA information can be obtained
at www.ICGtesting.com
Printed in the USA
LVHW031422170120
643976LV00001B/17